Know Money No

A Guide to Positive Personal Economics

Ronnie F. Lee

Book Cover Credits:

Photo by Devin Miles Lee
Art and graphics by Sergio Barbasso

Dedication

I want to dedicate this book to everyone involved in helping me out throughout my life. My life has been a tumultuous journey, and I would not have been able to survive it unless I had the support of my family and friends.

That is what you would expect me to say. Well, let me throw a wrench into your expectations right here. Life has been a blessing, but the road was full of obstacles. The blessing was having the mindset and tenacity to overcome those obstacles. My mantra has always been, *"I came into this world alone with an umbilical cord around my neck choking me out. I will step out of this world on my own as well!"*

To those who challenged me with their own insecurities, to those who thought college was necessary to achieve success, to those who criticized every choice I made and provided a list of reasons not to even try and succeed, this is dedicated to you. I am here to witness that when there is a will, and a little bit of know-how, there is a way!

Acknowledgment

I would like to thank my wife. She is never surprised by any of my crazy ideas. She has always been supportive and never underestimated me. I believe in me, so there is always someone who believes in me, but having a second person definitely helps with the heavy lifting.

About the Author

Ronnie F. Lee is truly a chapter out of the American dream. Born to a German mother who married an African-American man, who was enlisted in the Army, and raised in between the United States and Germany.

Even though both of Ronnie's parents worked and his father was actually a noncommissioned officer in the Army, he still felt the stress of a paycheck to paycheck environment. He felt the discomfort of countless cheese and mayo sandwiches six days before payday, and the disappointment of a dinner made up of mayo sandwiches without the cheese four days before payday.

The anger that comes with hunger when your father tells you to eat air-biscuits the night before payday. The joy of the first meal after payday, which is usually the family dining out. Ronnie recalls his father sitting down and showing him $900 that he received as an advance payment for the reassignment to a new duty station. He was mesmerized by the nine $100 bills and thought his family was just $100 short of being rich. His parents taught him a lot about economics. The lessons came through examples of what *not* to do, more so than by guidance and examples of what *to* do. To this day, neither of his parents own a home nor have substantial savings or assets. They went through foreclosures and car repossessions. His father even turned to stealing from Ronnie's savings to fuel his gambling obsession.

At the age of 11, Ronnie began doing odd jobs and established a lawn maintenance company without owning a lawnmower. He found opportunities at swap meets on the weekends and sold subscriptions to the Army Times during the week when he was 13 and 14. He left home and headed into the Army at the age of 18 with $125 and a backpack.

While in basic, he hustled and resold snacks, cards, batteries, and walkmans to generate enough revenue to not have to touch his very small paycheck. After discovering that his mother had taken that paycheck that he thought he was saving, he severed all economic ties with his mom and started over at the age of 18 with no money at all. Living in Italy for almost ten years, Ronnie built a career after the military in the music industry.

Managing himself as a functional illiterate in a foreign country, Ronnie worked hard, took advantage of opportunities that were presented, and created some opportunities out of thin air. Understanding the simple rules of supply and demand, the laws of what goes up must come down and clearly understanding what is needed and what is wanted, Ronnie returned to the

United States at the age of 32 with a net worth of $25,000. Since then, he has founded several small businesses, purchased a series of homes in the Las Vegas valley, placed his kids in private schools, and became a millionaire on two separate occasions.

Preface

'Know Money, No Problem' by Ronnie Lee is a captivating guide to help you better manage your daily expenses.

Our unstable finances have gripped us for too long. Families are constrained by their unstable finances to create a happy and healthy life for their children. How to escape these constraints? This book answers that question and more.

In Ronnie Lee's book, *'Know Money, No Problem,'* you will find the secrets to a life where you don't have to live paycheck to paycheck. Grab your copy of the book today.

Contents

Page Left Blank Intentionally

Chapter 1
Keeping It Real

People are driven by money. A majority of them seem to be driven by its allure. I continuously hear people talk about making more money so they can have a better lifestyle. Yet very few take the time to understand money. I think that even less have an understanding of how credit works and how detrimental debt can be.

Debt is a growing issue for workers. A quarter of workers (25%) have not been able to make ends meet every month in the last year, and 20% have missed a payment on some smaller bills. Furthermore, 71% of all workers say they're in debt — up from 68% last year (2019). While 46% say their debt is manageable, more than half of those in debt (56%) say they feel they will always be in debt. The real problem is that most of these people are in bad debt - the kind that brings with it anxiety, shame, and a lot of phone calls from collection companies. The point of this book is to help those 71% of workers who are in debt due to the choices they are making. Research conducted in 2017 concluded that the number of U.S households earning at least $100,000 had increased by 21.8%. It went from 7.4% in 2013 to 29.2% in 2017. It was also established that the median family income rose to between $50,000 and $74,000 for the majority.[1]

This shows that we are making more money and yet failing to work our way out of debt. This means that you will most likely be better served by gaining an understanding of the money you make rather than living paycheck to paycheck and hoping to win a lottery. There is always a chance that you will increase your revenue. I do not deny that fact. However, if you are like so

---

[1] https://www.cnsnews.com/news/article/terence-p-jeffrey/292-us-households-made-more-100000-2017

many other Americans, even when you increase your income, you will still be stuck in the loop of spending what you earn and then waiting for the next payday – if you don't know better! A 2017 CareerBuilder survey shows that 78% of people in the US live a paycheck-to-paycheck life, which is equivalent to 8 out of every 10 Americans.[2]

The odds are that these Americans cannot deal with a sudden health issue that brings with it a fat medical bill, the car not starting in the morning, which causes an unforeseen visit to the mechanic or an accident that is not fully covered by insurance. Living paycheck to paycheck also makes it very hard to save, and that is why 31% of people leading a paycheck-based life have

---

[2] http://press.careerbuilder.com/2017-08-24-Living-Paycheck-to-Paycheck-is-a-Way-of-Life-for-Majority-of-U-S-Workers-According-to-New-CareerBuilder-Survey

little to no savings.[3] Since America's workforce is more likely to be making $40,000 than $140,000, I want to share some of my own philosophies in regards to real-life economics. Even if you're making $15,000 per year and borrowed this book, you are making more than 10.7% of Americans or 30.57 million of the total US population.[4]

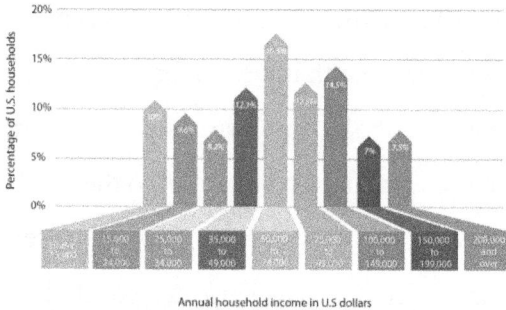

Annual household income in U.S dollars

[3] http://www.bankrate.com/banking/savings/financial-security-0617/

[4] https://www.statista.com/statistics/203183/percentage-distribution-of-household-income-in-the-us/

So, the question is, *"How did we get into this situation where we spend more than we make and fail to manage our income in an effective manner?"* To begin with, desire tends to have a greater impact than need in our society. People rationalize their way into a purchase they cannot truly afford or that they don't even need. The word of the day is, *"I want that."* Little do we realize that spending extra is not only linked with our financial management and stance, but it has a lot to do with the time that is invested in earning money that is spent sloppily. This is the essence of real-life economics, i.e., the relationship between time and money.

This is what we need to have a strong grip on in order to manage our lives better. There is a very fine line between buying things that we need and want and forcing ourselves into buying things that we can't afford just to keep up with the latest trend. Moreover, it is one thing to buy things that add to your overall utility and another to go on a spree of extravagance that leaves you in shambles financially. Sadly though, most Americans are guilty of the latter. As per a 2019 survey initiated by Ladder and carried out by One Poll, an average American spends around $1,497 per month on things that are not essential.[5] The yearly total of this monthly spending amounts to $18,000.

Yes, that's $18,000 that you could have saved or have used otherwise, but this is not it. It is not only about your financial investment but the investment of your time too. At $15 per hour, $18,000 requires 150 workdays of 8 hours each. That is almost six months of your life used for something you don't need, or maybe, you don't have the time to enjoy. The failure to prevent themselves from buying nonessential things and

---

[5] https://www.swnsdigital.com/2019/05/americans-spend-at-least-18000-a-year-on-these-non-essential-costs/

realizing the value of time in currency costs negatively impacts Americans in more ways than one. It causes not just a loss of money in the present but also undermines their future financial security as they fail to make investments and wise and timely economic decisions. The instant gratification of a new purchase apparently outweighs the rewards of long-term stability for many people. What does this really mean to us as individuals? A notable 38% of the total American population claim they can't afford to buy a retirement plan because of insufficient money or savings.

Moreover, a whopping 35% confirm that buying a life insurance policy is financially impossible for them, while 28% and 26% are struggling to pay off their credit cards and bear their car repairs, respectively.[6] What we actually lack here is the ability to say "*no*" to ourselves and the things that we know we can't afford yet still yearn for. The reason behind this could be anything from social acceptance to just satisfying your own desires. There are two ways we can keep ourselves from buying things we can't afford: (1) strengthening our willpower and (2) learning to build a relationship with money. When you are spending your hard-earned cash, make sure you truly know the price of your purchase. Money takes time to earn, and there is only so much time in our life cycle. You make sacrifices to earn your money.

You spend time away from loved ones, miss out on many hours of sleep, and may even have to do some things that are less than enjoyable. If

---

[6] https://www.forbes.com/sites/learnvest/2017/06/30/most-americans-are-taking-vacations-they-cant-afford/#e9d8c0a577ab

you're buying on credit you will actually be sacrificing your future time and sacrificing tomorrow for today's temporary high. This brings up another thing that plays a significant role in effective money management, and that is your relationship with money.

Yes, I did use the phrase *"relationship with money."*

Money, currency – or should we call it a note? – has only the value that society places on it. Individually, we each have a different relationship with money. Money can break marriages, crush families, or cause friends to become assassins. Technically speaking, money is a piece of paper that carries a value established by a centralized banking system and is used for trade of goods or services.

So, $100 is worth $100 of rocks, which may be 100 pounds of rocks today and only 90 pounds of rocks tomorrow. $5 may buy you a meal to fill the gap in your stomach, but if you ate a $100 bill, you would most likely remain hungry. Some people feel that money empowers them; it makes them feel important. Others think that it is a tool to leverage for other things they desire, like time, gifts, travel, and shelter, just to name a few.

Even then, there still are those who save money and stockpile it because it gives them a sense of security. The way one feels about money, the relationship they have with it will directly affect the way they manage it. While money is often regarded as the root of all evil, you simply can't deny that it also gives you the freedom of choice. And this is the very reason it is so important to maintain a healthy relationship with it.

By building a healthy relationship with money, I don't at all mean being rich or having a high purchasing power. Instead, I emphasize using it resourcefully and efficiently. If you try to "act" or "be" rich when you know you can't afford things that will help you look so, you are maintaining a poor relationship with your money. Ironically, you are trying to look wealthy, while you are racing to the poor house. You have tricked yourself into thinking your financial well-being comes from other people's perception rather than your own ability to manage your personal economic situation. If you don't want to make your relationship with money an abusive one, you must learn to spend money based on your values, goals, and needs. This is when you will start to value your money and learn to manage it well.

Ok, this is a great place for me to drop the disclaimer. I am not an accountant, nor have I studied economics inside the four walls of an accredited college. I have no financial background in stocks or bonds, have never worked at a bank, and the closest I have come to becoming an attorney is sleeping with one for the past decade. However, I do have real-life experience leaving home at the age of 17 with $125 in my pocket and working my way up to the 97th percentile in wealth. I feel I am the poster-child for the American average.

My father was in the US Army, where he retired after 20 years of serving this great nation. His discharge was honorable, but that does not mean that all his actions were. My mom is German, and she and my father actually met when he was stationed in Germany right after his two tours in Vietnam. My mother was a hard worker that totally fit the employee mold. She worked retail jobs as a clerk and was dedicated from 9 to whenever she was scheduled.

My father was stationed in different countries every 3 to 4 years, so we traveled between Germany and a different state in the US constantly. I went to elementary school on a military base in Kaiserslautern, Germany, a middle school in Killeen, Texas, the first three years of high school in Heidelberg, Germany, and graduated from a small school in Yermo, California. In my house, we did not talk about college.

We really did not talk about careers at all. I don't think we were very different from other American households. My parents never shared with me the rules of money. We did not talk about stocks, savings, assets, or equities. I was raised to be a worker, an employee for either a company or the government. I am sure it was to no one's surprise when I joined the US Army at the age of 18, seven months after graduating high school. Just like your average American soldier, I made $1.75 per hour.

I was able to secure a small $3,000-$4,000 after-the-tax signing bonus, which I kept in the bank through my entire enlistment. I took advantage of the benefits that allowed me to attend college courses, but I lacked the focus required for academics. I left the military five years in with an honorable discharge of my own and without a degree. I went back to the civilian world at the age of 23 in a foreign country, barely able to speak the language. I had discovered a path into the music industry while I was stationed in Italy, and I wanted to pursue it now. I was going to chase this opportunity even though it was not really my dream. Technically I was illiterate, a resident alien in my host country, and without a real job. I don't think it gets more average than that.

At the age of 32, I returned to America. I came back with $25,000, and I was starting over. I had been away from the US for over ten years. My credit was clean but had no depth. I had no records of purchasing a car, owning a phone, or even paying rent. I had one credit card with a

$1,500 limit. I had two friends in the city, and I had to sleep in my rented car while I was waiting for the office to open at the apartment complex where I had applied for an apartment. Four years after returning to the US and starting over, I moved into the second home I purchased. By the time I was 38, I was in the 90th percentile. I had multiple properties, drove nice cars, had money in the bank, and had no consumer debt. This was done by an average guy applying simple but not-so-average economics. I would like to share those simple economics with you.

What does the data say?

As per the Learn Vest Money Habits and Confessions Survey in 2017, 74% of people confirm that they have borne debts to cover the expenses of a vacation with the average debt amounting to $1,108. In another survey, 32% of Americans marked vacation budget planning as a more important financial priority than retirement planning. In fact, only 7% of respondents said they deem retirement planning more important than vacation planning. What's more surprising is that even with the increase in wages and a decline in mortgage rates, people residing in 70% of the country say they can't afford their own house. This 70% accounts for 335 counties out of a total of 473 in the United States. This is not all, though. Here are some more mindboggling facts when it comes to the buying decisions of Americans that consequently keep them from being able to invest in buying necessities like cars and houses.

As per the Fed Data, even though unemployment rates in the U.S have been on a decline since 1969, an estimated 4 of 10 people in the country struggle to bear emergencies amounting to merely $400. Likewise, 17% of people fail to pay their monthly bills, and about $1/4^{th}$ of the total population skipped essential medical care in the year 2018 because they couldn't afford it.[7] And yet, no one thinks of giving up vacations and associated debts. The situation is sad and dire, indeed. But this is how it is, and this is exactly where the fault lies.

"The amount of money you have has got nothing to do with what you earn. People earning a million dollars a year can have no money. People earning $35,000 a year can be quite well off. It's not what you earn; it's what you spend."

-Paul Clitheroe

---

[7] https://www.cbsnews.com/news/nearly-40-of-americans-cant-cover-a-surprise-400-expense/

Chapter 2
Money Matrix

If you are looking for a simple formula that you can apply and magically be financially healthy for life, I can give you that, and it is quite simple.

Don't spend money you don't have.

There you go. Put down the book, apply that rule, and you'll do fine.

A 2017 survey conducted by the Consumer Financial Protection Bureau (CFPB) on financial well-being found that approximately one-third of people between the ages of 30 and 49 have more credit card debt than savings.[8] For some, the reason behind overspending or spending money that one doesn't have in the first place is to be

---

[8] National Financial Well-Being Survey, Consumer Financial Protection Bureau, 2017

socially accepted and fill the perceived voids in their life. While for others, it can be an emotional appeal, an inability to control their desire to spend when there are too many choices, or simply thrills like sales and discounts. Regardless of the reason, you must work to exclude yourself from this lot of people who end up spending the money that they don't even own.

Now, if you're more like everyone else, this is a lot harder than it seems. Life brings with it situations that cause financial turmoil. We have desires, things that we want, and things we feel we need to have. We like to reward ourselves or help others when we really can't afford it.

All these things keep us from being able to apply the simple rule of *"Don't spend money that you don't have."* However, society does not set us up for that type of rule. A large portion of our society starts their adult life already in debt. They have been convinced to take large loans and give that money to big businesses called 'universities.' Ironically, the university gets paid whether or not the student gets a job after school. The student leaves with a debt that needs to be repaid and no guarantees.

That debt is money spent that the student did not have. It has been a decade or more since the great recession, but even today, the pupils in America can only achieve the bare minimum when it comes to their dreams. Most Americans in their 20s, 30s, and 40s say they feel privileged if they get a job after university that allows them to make loan payments.

For the 44 million students who gather the courage to borrow money to study and still owe money to pay, their ambitions and career goals have fallen prey to the burden of early debt. Speaking of student loans, a survey conducted by the Federal Reserve in 2017 revealed that greater student loans result in delayed marriages, and this hugely influences family planning. In addition, such debt lowers the odds of admission in graduate or professional degree programs and reduces the willingness of borrowers to accept low-paid public interest jobs. What's more, it even increases the dependency of children on their parents and the likelihood of living with parents for a long while, lowering the chances of borrowers ever being able to own their own homes.[9] However, school is not the only rule-breaker.

We buy cars, homes and sometimes even food on the money we have not yet earned. Americans do this so often that it does not even seem unique. It only becomes a problem when our income stream stops, and payments can't be made against our debt. We are set up in life to be in debt

---

[9] https://qz.com/1367412/1-5-trillion-of-us-student-loan-debt-has-transformed-the-american-dream/

– not necessarily working for the future, but more inclined to work for the past. The following is not as simple as the rule I mentioned before, but much more realistic. I call it *"The Money Matrix."* Generally speaking, money is no more than a token that is worked through a cycle. Money is either owed to you, due to someone else or sitting on standby.

The amount and timing of these three factors make up the matrix. The relationship between these factors is the difference between the lower, middle, and upper classes. As long as the money you have access to on stand-by or the money that is due to you is greater than the money you owe, you are rich. If not rich, you are at least financially healthy.

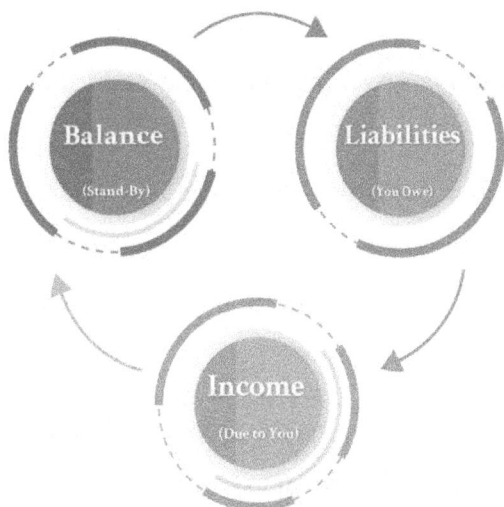

Money Matrix

Money can be due to you from a variety of sources; salary from your place of employment, annuities, loan repayment, and dividends, to name a few. This is the *"income"* portion of the money matrix. When allocating funds to this section, make sure you are talking about actual money that you receive. This is not the place to make projections or assumptions. Use hard numbers, and don't count on the money you have not actually secured. The money you owe others, such as non-asset purchases, car payments, rent, medical bills, and loan repayments, make up the *"liabilities"* portion of the matrix. Here, it is important to differentiate the money that is being invested and the money that's going down a one-way road.

Let me give you an example to clarify what I mean. When you pay rent, you are buying time in a particular space. You are not purchasing the actual space. When you pay a mortgage, you are actually buying the space along with paying for the time you are using other people's money to acquire the space. A portion of the mortgage, the interest, and the fees are a liability, and the remainder is actually building your balance. The money you have in savings, assets that are appreciating, stocks, and bonds are all part of the *"balance"* portion of the matrix.

The biggest asset that most American families will have is their home. When calculating the home as an asset, you will want to remember that all of your mortgage is not applied to the home. A large part of those payments is going to the mortgage holder as interest on your note. The way you manage the matrix and how you add to each section will either leave you a financial disaster or financially healthy and a fiscal minority in the United States of America. The one that wins the game is the one that has the most in the "*balance*" section of the matrix.

So here is the trick if you're short on time and don't want to read the whole book. Keep score of your financial health by adding entries into the three sections of the matrix: income, liabilities, and balance. Your focus is on transferring "*income*" into the "*balance*" section instead of the "*liability*" section. The more you are able to list in the balance sheet, the longer your wealth will last. Keep in mind that the interest that you pay is not listed in the *"balance"* section; it is a liability. Also, keep in mind that the money you think you're going to make but have not yet made does not count in the matrix.

Description	Category	Projected Cost	Actual Cost	Difference
Extracurricular activities	Children			$0
Medical	Children			$0
School Supplies	Children			$0
Movies	Entertainment	$50	$28 ▲	$22
Music (CDs, downloads, etc.)	Entertainment	$500	$30 ▲	$470
Sporting Events	Entertainment	$0	$40 ▼	($40)
Dining Out	Food	$1,000	$1,200 ▼	($200)
Groceries	Food	$100	$0 ▲	$100
Charity 1	Gifts and Charity	$200	$200	$0
Charity 2	Gifts and Charity	$500	$500	$0
Cable/Satellite	Housing	$100	$100	$0
Electric	Housing	$45	$40 ▲	$5
Mortgage or Rent	Housing	$700	$700	$0
Health	Insurance	$400	$400	$0
Home	Insurance	$400	$400	$0
Credit Card 1	Loans			$0
Credit Card 2	Loans			$0
Clothing	Personal Care	$150	$140 ▲	$10
Dry Cleaning	Personal Care	$0		$0
Health Club	Personal Care			$0
Food	Pets			$0
Grooming	Pets			$0
Medical	Pets			$0
Investment account	Savings or Investments			$0
Retirement account	Savings or Investments			$0
Federal	Taxes			$0
State	Taxes			$0
Bus/Taxi fare	Transportation	$100	$150 ▼	($50)
Fuel	Transportation	$450	$400 ▲	$50
Insurance	Transportation	$300	$300	$0

(Example of household budget template in Excel)

The matrix is not the only place to memorialize your finances. A budget is also a tool that I would like to recommend. You should know what you are spending and how you're distributing your earnings. Many people focus on what they make and forget to think about what they spend. Economics is all about "yin" and "yang": what you spend is the "*yin*" to what you make, which is the "*yang*." I have mentioned accounting for future income as an asset or part of your balance and that it should not be done.

I see this mistake made many times. You should not spend what you don't have since you never know what will happen or come up before you actually secure that income. That is like jumping out of the plane and hoping your friend will bring you a parachute on the way down.

"Financial peace isn't the acquisition of stuff. It's learning to live on less than you make, so you can give money back and have money to invest. You can't win until you do this."

-Dave Ramsey

Chapter 3
Holding On To Money

"Don't let go of what you don't have."

Watching so many of my friends and associates spend money before they actually have it in their possessions puts "holding on to money" at the top of my list of suggestions. I mentioned earlier that a lot of people rationalize purchases of the things they desire. This usually results in them spending tomorrow's income today.

This increases the numbers in the *"liability"* section of the matrix before adding anything to the *"income"* section, which, quite obviously, is not good. I run the risk of appearing like a helicopter parent when I ask you to not increase your spending because you think you will be making more money in the near future. Give yourself a window of time after receiving a pay increase or a windfall. Make sure you have actually received the bounty before spending it.

"Change how much you make, not how much you spend."

The best way to hold on to money is to maintain spending habits, even if your income increases. A study conducted by The Ascent Staff in March 2019 based on 1015 participants concluded that 76% of Americans are wasting money by paying an unnecessary fee for something while 73% are financing excessive or unnecessary interest.

In addition, 71% are impulsive buyers, 62% are using unneeded energy (gas, electricity), 51% are throwing out leftovers, and 46% are trashing items constantly because they are replacing old goods with new ones. And the list doesn't end here.[10] This is the reason I think that I know so many people that make much more than average but still live hand to mouth. They have limited items in their *"balance"* column and continue adding to their *"liability"* column. As soon as they make a few additional dollars, they want to buy a new car, take a trip or go out to eat at expensive restaurants. They impulsively feel the need to reward themselves.

This in itself would not be wrong, but they have done this their whole lives. So they are actually in debt and have already spent the additional funds they are now celebrating. The type of relationship these people have with money is that it is something to leverage and exchange for tangible items that bring them more joy. Perhaps they don't see it the way I do: the joy is temporary while the financial setback is

---

[10] https://www.fool.com/the-ascent/credit-cards/articles/study-the-most-wasteful-spending-habits-among-americans/

quite long-term. If you are not able to manage the money you make, you will always only be one month rich. I feel true wealth is a measure of time. You are as rich as the amount of time you can survive living the same lifestyle without additional funds in your *"income"* column through your active participation. True wealth is a positive relationship between time and income. Let's understand the reason behind it through this example:

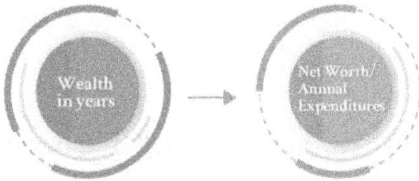

If we use this formula to measure the wealth of a millionaire having $4 million with a lifestyle that costs him around $2 million a year, the person in question will merely have two years of independence. On the other hand, if someone has

$250,000 and his lifestyle only requires $10,000 a year to complement social security, he will have 25 years of financial independence. This person might not even have the need to work anymore! While it generally appears that the millionaire who has $4 million and leading a luxurious life would be happier, research proved that such people can only be marginally happy.[11] A huge house and the latest posh cars might add value to their lives and bring happiness, but the fear and anxiety of eventually running out of money to support a lifestyle like theirs will always follow sooner or later.

If you have saved $120,000 and you spend $60,000 per year to manage your lifestyle, you are two years rich. If you stopped working and had no income generated from your *"balance"* column, you would be able to live for two years

---

[11] https://www.cbsnews.com/news/financial-wealth-its-time-not-money/

before you ran out of money. You could, of course, extend that time if you reduced the cost of living by modifying your lifestyle. Now the fact is that someone making $60,000 per year will probably not accumulate $120,000 worth of saving unless they never left home or if they continued to work well beyond the time that they have paid-off life's big-ticket items (e.g., furniture, real estate, student loans, etc.). So this person could offset their lifestyle expenses with passive income from their "*balance*" column.

These are stocks, bonds, dividends, rental income, or draws from business, to name a few. So, if this person with a $60,000 yearly lifestyle has $48,000 in their savings and has $3,000 in residual monthly income, they would be two years rich. This is a scenario that has a much better chance of being realized — a better chance, but still not very likely.

"Change what you spend on if you can't change what you make."

It is very important that you never rationalize yourself spending the money that you don't have to cover. A lot of times, we trick ourselves into believing that what we want is what we need. We try to keep up with the neighbors or make ourselves feel good with a material high.

Overspending is a situation that is much like walking down a long dark stairwell. Every step you take takes you further from the top, further from the light and deeper into the darkness. Every purchase that is made and dollar that is spent takes you deeper into debt and takes you further away from becoming financially healthy.

If your relationship with money is one that takes having money to make you feel secure, not having it will bring you a lot of anxiety. Empty pockets are quickly filled with stress, and the pleasure of what you purchased is very short-lived. This is where it is very important to apply the money matrix. Build your income bracket and avoid heading deeper in debt with money that you don't have. Money costs money, so keep in mind that when you buy on credit, you have to pay for what you purchased and the money you borrowed. If you have no way of increasing what you make, you have to decrease what you spend. Inventory your lifestyle; what are you driving? When are you driving? What are your utility costs, and where do you eat? Line up your money matrix.

If you are getting poor gas mileage, it may be time for a new car. Do an accounting of what your car is actually costing you to operate. I have spoken to people that have told me that they don't want to have to deal with a car payment or that they simply cannot afford one. Sometimes that is true but not always. If you have an older vehicle that gets 8 miles to the gallon, tends to need service every three months, and you were driving approximately 800 miles per month, your numbers would look a bit like this.

Gas	$300 per month
Repairs	$150 per month
Insurance	$80
Total cost	**$530**

If you were to drive a new vehicle that can cover 32 miles per gallon and has additional safety features and a warranty, your numbers would look more like this.

Gas	$75 per month
Repairs	$0 per month
Car Payment	$200
Insurance	$70
Total cost	**$415**

As you can see, you actually improve your money matrix by reducing your liabilities. You end up having $115 more of your income, thus increasing your financial health. This money is in your "*Income*" column and helps increase your net worth even though you have not made any more money. Take a look at when you eat, where you eat, and what you are spending on food. If you're addicted to gourmet coffee at $5.50 a cup and eating lunch or dinner at a restaurant almost daily, rethink this type of expense. A cup of coffee made at home can reduce the daily coffee expense by $4 a day. Bringing in your lunch from home can also reduce your expenses from $7 to $18 down to $3 or $4. That would impact your monthly liabilities by $80 per month.

This is not for everyone. This may not even be necessary if you already have your matrix heavily weighted towards the "*income*" or "*balance*" column. This type of process is good when there is a tilt towards the "*liability*" column. If you can't make more money, use the money you have, smarter.

Chapter 4
Spending Money Wisely

"Money on a grill burns but provides you nothing to eat."

Money is part of a cycle. You invest your time to make it and then use it to pay for other people's time. Keep this in mind when you're spending your money. The money you are spending represents the time it took you to make it. I am sure you know of more than one person who has to work extended hours to keep up with all the desired toys they tend to purchase.

They have the most up-to-date technology when it comes to TVs and sound systems, have an ATV in the garage, a weight room with all of the weights and cardio equipment to train, a small basketball team, and a computer in every room. The problem is, they have no time to take advantage of any of these things. They are burning money, putting little to nothing into the "*Balance*" column, and forcing themselves to have to work more and harder. Spending money wisely has more to do with understanding what money costs than anything else.

There is no need to spend every dime you make. Choose your purchases based on priorities. You should make sure that you have paid your past debt before creating more debt. You should first make sure your needs are met before purchasing accessories. I highly recommend that you buy some time. This is done by putting money aside or purchasing those items that can be added to the "*balance*" column.

"Money in your account is better than money in theirs."

A lot of people do not understand the value of leasing a vehicle instead of purchasing. They tend to get stuck on the desire to own. When I ask people with good credit why they are purchasing their vehicle, a lot of them will say: *"Because you don't ever own the car."* My response is that you don't ever own the car because you never pay for it! Let me be clear; leasing a vehicle is not for everyone. If you drive a lot of miles, tend to damage your car excessively, or want to keep your next car for more than seven years, a lease is not for you. You can go ahead and drive a $30,000 car paying $566 per month for 60 months.

Your warranties will most likely end after the last day of your fourth year, which is when, coincidentally, that you will start having mechanical issues. This will take more money out of your pocket while you're still paying for your car that is actually depreciating day after day. You will have paid $33,960 for a car that may ultimately be valued at $10,000 if you're lucky. Now you can drive your old car without payments. It will not cost you any more money than standard maintenance, as its value continues to depreciate. The good thing is now you can use the money you're not spending on the car to invest in your "*balance*" column. The bad news is you did not have the use of the cash flow until five years into the deal.

Depending on the make and model of the car you leased, the scenario could be a bit more like this: You use the car just like it was your own for 36 months, paying about $410 per month. The car will be under warranty for the full term of your lease, so you will have no extra maintenance costs.

You will spend $14,760 and keep $5,616 in your own account during the 36-month term. In the matrix, money is time, and this provides you more time. You also do not have to pay the balance of $15,240 for an old car.

"Don't add water to a bucket that is already full."

One day we had a leak in the kitchen. I called a plumber, and he found that my reverse osmosis system was leaking under my kitchen sink. It had been leaking for days, and the damage was extensive. The repairs included the disassembling of my counters and cutting out a part of my wall. My wife and I thought we would use this occasion to do a little bit of remodeling.

We called on a few people to provide us a bid on replacing our kitchen cabinets, countertops and redoing the floors downstairs. The price would be approximately $30,000. My wife was excited and ready to pick out colors. My mind went in the opposite direction, and we started looking for a new house.

If you're confused, give me a second to explain. I lived in a community that was very hard hit by the bubble of 2008. Home prices had been slashed by up to 60%. Most of the homes on my street were underwater. My house was probably priced in the top 5%. I bought it late and added a lot of upgrades, which pushed my price up. I knew that my home would be brought down by the comparable home sales, not up. $30,000 invested in my home would be like dropping a lot of money down a hole in the back yard. This investment would not increase the value of my home dollar per dollar. In fact, I doubt it would increase the value of my home at all, but I would personally be short of $30,000.

A down payment on a new house in 2015 was approximately 5% if you had good credit. I had excellent credit by simply following the concepts laid out in this book. The math was very simple: $30,000 was the down payment on a $600,000 house. I just needed to find the right house. I needed to find something that was in the early stages would have some built-in price increases by the builder and was in an area that was appreciating well.

"Search, and you will find." We did just that. We found a home in a community that was appreciating at a rate of approximately 9% and was due to have at least two price increases in the development, which would be approximately $20,000 each. My wife had faith in me, but she still did not fully understand, so I had to explain it.

The $30,000 paid to remodel our home would be an expense. The money would be spent, and we would have nice floors and a great kitchen but no added value. The new home would require a $30,000 investment. This was not an expense since the money would be sitting in the equity of the new home.

We would acquire a $600,000 asset that would gain approximately $40,000 before we closed and $54,000 in appreciation by the end of the first year. There was a very good chance that my balance sheet would increase by $94,000 by buying a new house. If I fixed up the house I was in, my balance sheet would actually decrease by $30,000, and my net worth would, consequently, also decrease. Three years after we purchased that new home and added a pool, the home value had appreciated to $840,000. My balance sheet had increased by $150,000.

"A dollar today can save you $100 next week."

Preventive investment is much like preventive maintenances on your car and equipment. Back when I was in the Army, we had to make sure that we took a look at our equipment before using it, and periodically, an in-depth inspection was scheduled.

This was because Uncle Sam knew it was a lot cheaper to check and see if there was oil in the engine rather than running the engine without oil and blowing it up. Sure, these inspections cost time and a little bit of money, but they saved a lot of money in the long run. Preventive investment is money spent today to avoid greater expenses tomorrow. Think of it like brushing your teeth. You have to pay for toothpaste and take time to brush. This is an investment to prevent tooth decay, which could eventually cost you thousands of dollars. So you spend a few dollars a month on the tools and toothpaste. We take our car in to be looked at when the check engine light comes on— or at least we should. We wash our hands to try and avoid the potential cold or flu.

When considering yourself as an individual or as part of a family, preventative planning can go a long way. The fewer benefits our employer provides, the fewer extras we have on the side to help us out when trouble hits.

This means more attention should be applied to preventative investment. It is basically money used today to reduce the impact of future expenses. There are a lot of people without health insurance and just as many without life insurance. Illness and death are much more detrimental when they cause an ongoing financial hardship for those left behind. Knowing that you do not have a plan in place for these occurrences, which are almost guaranteed to occur, is like riding a motorcycle really fast without a helmet down a curvy road in a rainstorm, blindfolded.

I totally understand that with the current price of health insurance, it may not be possible to secure coverage for everyone. Health insurance in and of itself is very costly, and it is a sure payment that you will make whether you need medical attention or not.

My family pays in excess of $8,000 a year in health insurance, and we rarely see a doctor. We can afford not to since if we do have a medical issue, we are insured. We pay for insurance instead of making the preventative investment. For those that do not have health insurance, I strongly recommend making a preventative investment. That means seeing a doctor every year, do regular checkups, and make sure you don't do anything too crazy as far as diet and high-risk activities. In fact, practice some good eating habits, pay attention to what you consume, avoid known health risks, and exercise regularly. In case of a vehicle, use a good source of fuel, check your oil, and maintain your tire pressure.

If you own your home, change the air filters in your cooling/heating system. If you have breakers that pop, find out why before you have a major issue, don't light up empty space, fix any and all leaks as soon as they appear. Don't use HVAC when not at home and consider alternative energy.

I was reluctant to add solar powers to my home, but after crunching some numbers, the deal was too good to walk away from. I signed a contract, the company came out and installed a massive solar system, and I did not pay a dime. I received a guaranteed amount of kilowatts per year at a fixed price for 20 years, and suddenly, I started to get negative power bills from the utility company. For those of you who have a few assets and don't have life insurance while carrying debt— wake up and smell the coffee.

Just because you have no plans for dying does not mean you will not die. Think of your loved ones, especially if you are the main income earner. How will they be able to deal with their loss while they also have to deal with a mortgage they can no longer afford, the car payment, tuition, and paying to bury you? Research shows that an average American dies with a debt of $62,000.[12] That is probably going to remain the same for us, and we will all die, leaving debt

---

[12] https://www.cbsnews.com/news/americans-are-dying-with-an-average-of-62k-of-debt/

behind for our loved ones to deal with. Is that what we really want? Of course not! What is saddest is that most Americans leave this situation behind unwillingly, and the reason is that they spend money they haven't earned, thinking they will catch up tomorrow. Tomorrow, however, is not guaranteed.

Another study conducted by the Credit Reporting Agency, Experian, based on 2016 data and shared with Credit.com, confirms that 73% of consumers in America die while still having dues and debts.[13]

The consumers included in this sample were those who had an average total of $61,554 due when they died, inclusive of mortgage debt. If we take mortgage out of the equation, the average per person debt left behind after death is $12,875.

---

[13] https://www.cbsnews.com/news/americans-are-dying-with-an-average-of-62k-of-debt/

While it is true that mortgage and home loans; in fact, *all* debt that is taken to build a home or business or for other constructive purposes, is good, not planning to address it and failing to plan how your family will fare in case you aren't there anymore, is detrimental.

You wouldn't want to live a life building a home and die with debts attached to your name, would you? Leaving your loved ones to shoulder the burden of your debt after you're gone completely counteracts the 'good' that is attached to these investment vehicles.

Instead of earning assets that you can have in your name, you earn debt, which likely increases with each delayed payment and for which your loved ones are forced to bear the effect. And the sole culprit here is you for being unable to prepare or simply not being able to save up for unforeseen events.

Chapter 5
Manage Your Debt

"Don't eat all your eggs before you raise a chicken."

Most of us will have to deal with debt at one time or another. Some of us have been spending money before we made it. From an early age, we start borrowing a few dollars here and there. It can be debt from a friend while at the movies, or money from our parents that we use to purchase something we want while at a store or when we want to subscribe to something like a magazine, club, or gym.

In this case, we settle the situation by telling them they can deduct it from our allowance/pocket money. Later in life, most of us experience situations where we find ourselves walking across the university campus, and someone with a fold-up table tells us they will give us a T-shirt and $1500 to spend anywhere we want with small monthly payments to pay it back. Anytime you purchase something without the money to pay it in full at the time of purchase, you are adding to your liability column and taking on debt. When it comes to money, debt can also be measured as time. I'm sure you have heard the saying *"time is money."* Well, money also buys time.

Generally speaking, wealth is a matter of time. Employees trade their time for money. And those who have money, exchange it with others to have more of their time. We can always make more money, but we can never make more time. When you take on greater debt, you are eating away at your time. The relationship between time and money also goes like this: If you put in the effort and time, you can always make more money, but you can't get more time regardless of how much money you spend to get it.

In this manner, when you are having someone else purchase something for you or pay for you using their money with the promise that you will pay them back over time, you are selling your time. Usually, in this case, they are allowing you the use of their money because you will be paying them back more than they paid you in the first place.

This way, you're increasing the value of their time. Simply put, this increase is what we call *"interest."* This is a kind of penalty that you bear because you cannot or do not wish to wait to make the purchase with your own money. The penalty is the extra amount that you have to pay on top of what you actually borrow and how you tie your future up, trying to pay down the purchase price. One way you can offset this burden is by being aggressive with your repayment and reducing the amount of time you are in debt.

This will also reduce the amount of debt that you have to pay back as long as there are not any financial penalties or other conditions that prohibit you from saving money (pre-payment penalties, for example). Managing your debt can make a major difference in your money matrix. As I mentioned before, your debt will come with a price tag. Depending on who is providing you with the credit, you may be paying anywhere from 1.9% to 24%. The overall effect of the cost associated with your debt is further affected by the amount of time that debt is open.

One of the problems some people have is not one big purchase but many small purchases that they really could not afford, so they sell their future to make a purchase. Long-term debt is usually associated with big-money deals. For example, you purchase a home for $200,000 on a 30-year fixed loan with 6% interest. Once all is said and done, and if you make your 360 scheduled payments, you will have paid approximately $431,000 for your property once you add $231,000 interest or fee for using other people's money over time. If you understand this debt/time relationship thoroughly, it will better prepare you to manage it. Let me give you another example.

The $200,000 property that we discussed would cost you $83,000 less if you paid an extra $215 per month. It would also only take you 20.5 years to pay off the debt, instead of 30 years that it stretched up to in the first scenario. The shorter the amount of time, the lesser is the cost that you bear for using other people's money over time.

It is true that in the above example, you will pay an additional $52,890 over a 20.5-year spread due to the increased payments. However, paying a little more every month cut off almost ten years of payments, ultimately allowing you to save a massive chunk of change. This is how you save time and money by using your own money to pay for other people's money. What you spend is what you can utilize for better purposes. This is your true wealth because both of these things combined allow you to experience life better.

Like Henry David Thoreau says: *"Wealth is the ability to fully experience life."*

Imagine how that amount of money and time that you save could affect your life positively. The trick is you have to not overload yourself with small-time debt, which prohibits you from paying the additional $215 towards your mortgage each month.

On a side note, an aggressive repayment plan on a home will increase the chance that your equity will stay ahead of interest, building your numbers in the *"balance"* column much faster. As a rule of thumb, you can avoid paying over time, if that time is associated with a fee. Make your money and apply it to your *"balance"* column. When the time comes to make a purchase, use the money you have already made instead of committing to the money you still don't have. When you do have to create a debt that comes along with interest, be very aware of the time factor. Pay down on the principal as aggressively as possible. Pay off the debt with higher costs associated with it first and never agree to debt that comes with early repayment penalties.

"Don't pay for a steak and then leave it on the plate."

Let's talk about credit cards. Most of us have credit cards, but only some of us can manage them well. As per a 2017 report compiled by Experian, a conventional American has 3.1 credit cards on average, a credit card balance of $6,354, and a credit score of 675.[14] Credit cards are a

---

[14] https://www.businessinsider.com/credit-card-use-across-the-us-2018-8

great safety belt, but just like a safety belt, you really don't want to have to use them since that means there has been a wreck. The best way to use a credit card is in place of cash. A good credit card has built-in features that can protect you from loss of your purchases and provide you with additional benefits.

These benefits can actually save you money. For example, when you rent a car, your credit card may cover the additional insurance requirements. Just like money, these cards are also related to time. When you purchase something on the card, someone else (the bank) is actually paying for your purchase.

The bank then extends the amount of time for you to pay them back. They charge you for this time and usually at a rate that is much higher than a mortgage. They also tend to only ask you to pay a minimal margin above the principle. This causes the liability to linger and increase how much you pay, and they profit. Credit card companies also allow you to do balance transfers or take cash advances. Sometimes they allow these transactions to be combined with a period of time for which they do not apply interest, as long as you make the minimum payments. Most of the time, when you take advantage of these balance transfers, there is an upfront fee associated with the transaction.

This fee can vary but is usually between 2% and 6%. Balance transfers typically do not have additional interest applied to them. Cash advances, on the other hand, generally are accompanied by the highest interest rates that you're charged by your respective card providers.

Keep in mind that if you take advantage of a balance transfer that has an upfront fee applied, you have already paid the interest on the full amount for the agreed time. So, for example, if you do a balance transfer that comes with a 5% transfer fee, but offers zero-interest for the first 12 months, the predefined fee (5%) takes the place of your standard interest that you would otherwise pay against your credit card debt. However, it is applied to the full principle. This way, if you don't take advantage of that time period (the 12 months of interest-free payments), you also pay for the time that you did not use. So, since you have already purchased the time when using these options, I would recommend you use it. In other words, there's no reason to aggressively pay-off this particular debt.

If you have additional funds, pay accounts that are applying interest on the principal first. Credit cards have become a very big part of economic freedom. The problem is that they are a bit addictive, and like everything else that you get addicted to, things can get out of hand very quickly when using credit cards.

Managing your credit cards is a bit like managing other people's money as if it were your own. Time is the key, and understanding the terms that come along with your card is essential. To cut the discussion short, credit cards are great tools if you know how to use them properly. If you pay off the purchases before the end of the grace period, it truly is free money for you. The amount of interest on the card does not matter if the interest is never applied.

One thing that you should remember when choosing a credit card is that you get one that comes with additional features, such as extended insurance, loss replacement, and rewards for purchases made. On the other hand, one thing that you should never opt for and don't even want to do is own a card that comes with an annual fee. Credit card companies are competitive and make lots of money from the merchants they provide services to. There is no reason for you to pay them on top of the money they are already making on every purchase you make. Let me close by making sure I reiterate — or say if I have not said it already — credit cards are trump cards when it comes to leveraging your financials. One of the best ways to build your credit profile is with credit cards. So, make sure you secure one as soon as you can.

Use it to make purchases, but nothing beyond what you can pay for at the end of the month. The Credit Card Act of 2009 mandates that all credit card companies grant their customers a "grace period," which can be no less than 21 days (usually scheduled between 21-25 days for most major credit cards) during which no interest can be charged. You should, therefore, pay off your before the end of the grace period, thus avoiding interest altogether. You also want to avoid maxing cards out. It is better to have three credit cards with a $2,000 limit each and carry $1,000 of debt on each of them than to have one card maxed out at $2,000. Available unused credit shows that you have controls in place and good money management skills. Banks like to see that and will reward you with a higher credit score because of it.

"Sometimes, the wrench works as a hammer."

Credit cards have more than one function and can be used in several ways. They don't just create debt; they also help manage it. When you become the victim of a sinkhole in your *"Liability"* column, you need to get creative. Your primary focus should be to reduce the cost of time and then reduce the principal of your debt. If your interest payments are too high, you are hardly able to make a dent on your actual outstanding debt. Having credit cards on standby that you keep without a balance can be a great wrench to use as a hammer. These cards, when well-managed, actually compete for your business.

They will offer you perks such as 2% balance transfers. This can be a great tool in getting your finances back on track, provided you use it wisely and correctly. Let's end this chapter with another example that will help you better understand how credit cards work. Suppose you have a credit card with a $5,000 balance and an 18% interest rate.

You're paying about $75 per month against the interest alone, which means your $150 payment is actually only reducing your principle by approximately $75. If you set up a balance transfer with a 2% upfront fee, your principle will increase to $5,100. From that point forward, your full $150 will be applied to the principle, greatly reducing the amount of time it takes to pay down the debt. In this manner, you no longer pay for the time by the day, and you get one step closer to good financial health.

Chapter 6
Making Money Work

"Don't exchange a quarter for two dimes."

We have reached chapter six of the book, but I am going to say it again. Economics is a measure of time. Time and money are two sides of the same coin. To make your money work for you, it is important that you pay attention to this fact. Smart choices and an understanding of the matrix can make the difference between having one day or one lifetime worth of wealth.

I have had conversations with smart individuals that explain to me that they have a five- or six-thousand-dollar credit card debt with ten thousand dollars in the bank. Sometimes, they are holding on to the credit card debt with the same bank that they have deposited their money into.

That is kind of like Paul asking Peter to hold on to his money and Peter offering to pay him one penny per $10 that he holds on to. Then Paul wants to make a purchase but does not want to ask Peter for his own money back, so he agrees to use Peter's money and pay him 40 cents for every $10 Peter lets him borrow. Paul is paying for the time he has Peter's money at a rate of 4% interest.

Peter is only paying Paul for the money he is holding at 0.01% interest. Now here comes the kicker; it's the same money! Peter gave Paul his own money back to use for his purchase, and Paul is paying him 4% to use his own money. I guess it's all the same because if Paul did not use the money, Peter would give it to Joe and still make 3.99% on Paul's money while Paul is not even keeping up with inflation. You should really reconsider if you are paying to use someone else's or your own money over time while having someone else hold onto your capital. That is not the best way to make your money work. The simplest way to make your money productive is to use it in place of other people's money that you have to pay for over time. Don't pay interest on the money you have liquid and available. If you have cash in hand, you should not be paying for someone else's money while receiving little to nothing for yours.

But this does not mean you should not have access to liquid emergency funds. It simply means you have to make sure you are not depleting your own funds beyond what is necessary. Let's have a quick flashback to the link between relationships with money. The person that keeps a lot of money in a checking or savings account is usually the type of person that feels money keeps them safe and secure. They would rather carry the burden of low interest paid by their bank, with little to no gain, than to be without money because they simply feel vulnerable if they do not have access to capital.

"The way to fill a bucket is by keeping more inside of it than outside."

There are a variety of ways to make money and just as many ways to keep it. We have hit on a few and will most likely cover some more before the end of this book. One thing I will ask you to always consider is the long-term effect of your daily financial choices.

Once again, it is the relationship between time and money, and when your money is meant to work for you, your time should be considered. Position your money where it grows with time. This can be in stocks, business ventures, bonds, loans, foreign currency, real estate, art, or collectibles. The usual rule is that the more at-risk your money is, the more your time in that position will be worth. At this point, you are probably saying, *"I don't want to risk losing my money."* But what you are actually doing is risking increasing your money. To be clear, keeping your money in a savings account that pays you 0.01% and is secured is a sure way of losing money. Even if there were a 1% inflation rate, your money would have less buying power at the end of each year, and time would definitely not be on your side.

You're losing money because of fear and the lack of a big-picture perspective. Don't get me wrong, but you have got to be conservative and take an educated risk. You must know how much exposure you can handle. In the words of Grant Cardone, the famous millionaire;

"Save to invest, don't save to save. The only reason to save money is to invest it."

So, do not just play safe by keeping your money in a bank and thinking it is working for you. Work to make your money work for you. That's when you will be able to make the most of it.

"The wind is always blowing somewhere."

A word to remember here is *"residual income."* When it comes to the matrix, we place this in the *"balance"* bucket, and it acts as a never-ending well, feeding your *"income"* column. There are multitudes of ways to create residual income from royalties, annuities, interest revenue, and business ownership.

Sometimes life gets in the way of opportunities, and you have to measure your risk when trying to set up your residual income. The funny thing here is that a lot of people don't even think about creating residual income. We are all being told since our childhood to save money as someday we will have to retire. The problem with this is you will have to be able to save enough money to maintain your lifestyle for twenty or thirty years. Granted, you may receive social security or even some type of pension, which in and of itself is a residual income.

If you play your cards right, pay off all of your debt, and downsize the last stages of your life, you will win.

If you have set up additional revenue streams that provide you income without a need for you to be proactive in generating that income, that buys time; a lot of time, for you to be able to continue living life without the stress of money.

Chapter 7
Build on Solid
Foundation

"Know what's in the hole before you jump into it."

According to the credit reporting agency Experian, student loan debt reached an all-time high of $1.4 trillion in 2019's first quarter. The stats show an upsurge of 8% from 2018 and a staggering increase of 33% since 2014 – a time when student debt was $1.06 trillion.

With the current financial situation regarding student debt, it wouldn't come as a surprise if the figure soared to $2 trillion by 2024.[15] These figures have put a strain on the U.S. financial

---

[15] https://www.experian.com/blogs/ask-experian/state-of-student-loan-debt/

economy, and it is one of the major contributors to the growing debt load. It is also the second-largest source of credit debt for Americans. However, the increasing cost of obtaining a higher education is the reason why students and their parents are assuming student debts.

Obtaining a degree in today's world is a huge financial outflow, and as per the College Board, the average expenditure to attend a public four-year institution has increased three times in the past three decades and doubled for a private four-year degree.[16]

Savings and investments alone cannot suffice for the soaring costs, and it's high time that students lay their financial goals on a strong base so that they can save for a secure future. According to a study carried out by the Institute

---

[16] https://research.collegeboard.org/trends/college-pricing/highlights

for College Access & Success, seven in ten college graduates who are seniors owe around $30,000 in student debt.[17] The Federal Reserve has reported an outstanding student debt of more than $1.5 trillion, and the situation demands some concrete solutions to help American students to swim out of this vicious cycle of circular debt.[18]

The millennial generation is in desperate need of some surefire financial remedies, as 87% of them have reported being broke in the past or report being currently broke.[19] The next step to evaluating what can be done to address your student loan debt is to categorically identify the loopholes (e.g., deferrals, forbearances, debt forgiveness for working in the public service

---

[17]https://www.cnbc.com/2015/11/13/its-time-to-get-an-education-on-student-loan-options.html
[18]https://www.federalreserve.gov/releases/g19/HIST/cc_hist_me mo_levels.html
[19] https://www.creditloan.com/blog/broke-in-america/

sector, etc.) and divert your energy and resources where they are otherwise most required. This will put you in better control of your financial future so that you can begin repaying your college loans before they start taking a toll on your financial well-being. I have had more conversations with students than I can count, which were at least ¾ based on no facts at all. Such students have no idea of how they are going to own up to their finances. They simply put themselves in debt to seek higher education with blind faith that employment is inevitable. Surprisingly, these graduates even overestimate the salaries that they expect to receive after they graduate.

A study cited this over-expectation by 23%, where 1,000 students representing college grads were surveyed to give an honest salary expectation for no-experience opportunities as well as at a mid-career level.[20] Another College Pulse survey by LendEDU revealed student expectations and how they are not being met.[21] PayScale has come to the conclusion that a typical graduate having zero to five years of experience is most likely to have an average salary of $48,400 and the average starting salary for 2018 graduates, according to The National Association of Colleges and Employers (NACE) was $50,004.[22] [23]

---

[20] https://www.inc.com/minda-zetlin/college-grads-overestimate-starting-salaries-study-shows.html
[21] https://lendedu.com/blog/college-graduates-salary-expectations-realities
[22] https://www.naceweb.org/job-market/compensation/class-of-2018s-preliminary-starting-salary-shows-slight-drop/

[23] http://collegepulse.com/

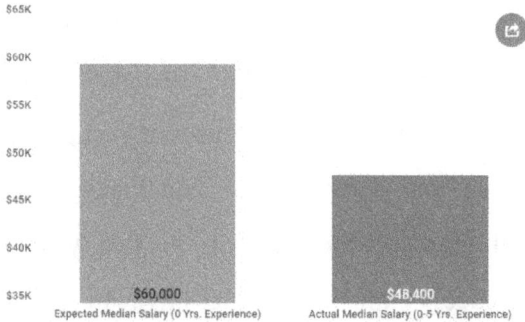

One of the most wonderful things that modern times present us with is an opportunity. We have plenty of opportunities that we can avail ourselves of and have more access to resources than ever before. All you need is a vision, an executable idea, and an undying spirit to achieve the impossible. A financially responsible individual would have adopted certain habits that will enable them to stay steadfast on their journey to financial independence Laying a strong foundation is not only important but an absolute necessity in today's fast-paced and stressful world with the ever-increasing financial costs of living a decent life going through the ceiling.

Thus, wake up from your slumber and start taking practical steps towards a financially secure future.

Build Your Balance Sheet!

The first step in taking responsibility for your finances is to have a fair idea of where you stand in terms of what you own and what you owe. Setting up an account of your assets and liabilities might take considerable time and effort the first time, but it will be worth it in the long run. Building a personal balance sheet encompasses listing down your assets, such as:

- Fixed assets: a house, car or a piece of land that you own
- Any tangible or intangible investments
- Account balances
- Jewelry
- Or any other personal belongings having a considerable liquid value

Your liabilities, on the other hand, include credit card debt, mortgages, or different kinds of debts such as personal, student, or auto loans. Having a summary of your net worth in terms of liquid and non-liquid assets and liabilities gives you a road map on how to balance it with your income and track cash flow.

"A budget allows you to know your cash flow, which guarantees you aren't overspending."

-Erin Lowry (Author of "Broke Millennial: Stop Scraping by and Get Your Financial Life Together")

Devise a budget around how much you own and owe and tie it in with automatic contributions and stick to it so that you see a substantial change in your financial situation over time. Moreover, check your numbers and have a plan in writing. Don't simply say you want to live a better life. You need to be in conscious control of your finances and avoid blaming external factors so that you can have your financial life together.

Debts Are Financially Taxing – Get Rid Of Them

Did you know that 60 to 70% of individuals in the age bracket of 18-34 years still depend on their parents for their financial "independence" as per MarketWatch?[24] And guess what? The major dependence is due to insurmountable **student debt loans**, rising rents, and the exorbitant costs of living coupled with rising inflation and stagnant wages.

Debts are like pests who chip away at your financial strength and ultimately leave you under undue pressure. Therefore, building a strong financial foundation entails being holistically aware of the factors that are draining your

---

[24] https://www.marketwatch.com/story/why-its-time-to-cut-millennials-some-slack-for-being-financially-dependent-on-their-parents-2019-07-16

financial health.

The best way to get rid of them is to allocate a certain part of your income to clearing your debt so that they do not haunt you later on. Tap into your savings before taking on more debt as 43% of college costs are covered through savings according to a 2019 report.[25] However, if you want to eliminate the already accumulated debt, get organized, pick up a suitable payment plan, and resist the urge to spend on your credit card.

Expand Your Savings through Sustainable Investments

Knowing your financial situation and planning well in advance for a financial emergency is something every financially responsible person would consider taking up.

---

[25] https://www.salliemae.com/about/leading-research/how-america-pays-for-college

These include plans like:

Maintaining an emergency fund

It's always advisable to have a contingency plan in place for a rainy day as mishap doesn't befall with prior notice. Follow a step-by-step process to set up an emergency fund commensurate with your financial standing, which can keep you covered in times of financial crisis such as the loss of a job, an unexpected expense, or other uncalled for financial crises. A small investment in the present can keep you prepared for a rainy day. You've just got to figure out what works for you and what doesn't.

Insurance can be a lifesaver

It is advisable to procure insurance policies that cover your major medical costs, sudden deaths, and any uncertain losses caused by fire or fraud. Seriously consider insuring your pets if you are attached to them. I once received a puppy for my birthday. The dog ended up eating a sock, which cost me over $6,000 to remove, and that was within three months of receiving this wonderful gift and, unfortunately, before I placed insurance on him. These out-of-pocket expenses can be debilitating and cause you to reconsider your budget and lifestyle. So if you want to be prepared beforehand, it's better to have yourself insured lest you have to bear the brunt of extraordinary expenses. These are just a few actionable tips for you to follow to help better manage your funds, but in the end, it's all about how consistent you are in your spending and saving habits.

Inculcating a good habit is only sustainable in the long run if you regularly re-evaluate your financial journey and keep track of the possible leaks that could be draining your savings. In the end, set SMART and realistic financial goals so that you don't fall back on them and get stuck in a guilt trip for not being able to manage your finances well.

Your actions define you, and taking practical steps towards financial independence shapes your personality and perspective on life. What we do need to realize is that every individual has their own unique needs and preferences, which will ultimately inform the customization of their financial plan.

"One size does not fit all."

Keeping up with the Joneses can cause you to lag on your savings standards. However, is your poor financial situation due to increasing debt? Or are you able to maintain a well-thought-out and balanced personal budget? Nobody knows your life situation better than you.

Personal finance rules-of-thumb are an efficient and effective way to achieve financial success as they help you devise a strategy around your unique needs.

According to the U.S. Census Bureau's 2017 data, around 17.5% of Americans are under student loans, and an additional 2017 CNBC article reaffirms that 44 million students have an outstanding student loan debt.[26] [27] Hence, if you are a student struggling to get your finances in shape and being burdened by the ever-increasing student loan, it is high time that you take charge of your finances.

---

[26] https://www.census.gov/quickfacts/fact/table/US/PST045218
[27] https://www.cnbc.com/2017/02/17/credit-card-users-rack-up-over-1-trillion-in-debt.html

PERCENTAGE OF BUDGET

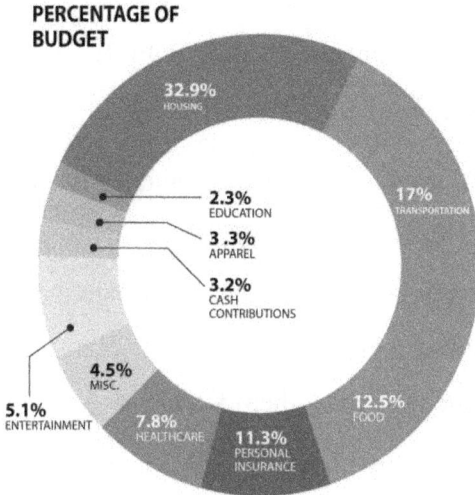

32.9% HOUSING

2.3% EDUCATION

3.3% APPAREL

3.2% CASH CONTRIBUTIONS

17% TRANSPORTATION

4.5% MISC.

5.1% ENTERTAINMENT

7.8% HEALTHCARE

11.3% PERSONAL INSURANCE

12.5% FOOD

[28]

Financial literacy is critical to stay on top of your savings and ensure your financial well-being. According to a study by the National Endowment for Financial Education, only a meager 24% of millennials are financially

---

[28] https://www.debt.com/statistics/

literate.[29] In addition to that, 56% of millennials do not have any savings set aside for their retirement. The scenario for Baby Boomers and Gen-Xers is only a bit better at 39%.[30]

The stats are shocking and only indicate poorer financial accountability, with 20% of Americans not having any saving plan in place.[31] And those who actually do save aren't putting aside enough to last them for the long term.

---

[29] https://www.nefe.org/press-room/news/default.aspx
[30] http://www.prnewswire.com/news-releases/research-from-purepoint-financial-shows-the-american-dream-is-changing-as-savings-stagnates-300525715.html
[31] https://www.cnbc.com/2018/03/15/bankrate-65-percent-of-americans-save-little-or-nothing.html

What percentage of annual income do you save?

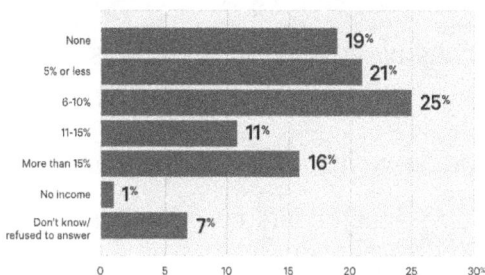

None	19%
5% or less	21%
6-10%	25%
11-15%	11%
More than 15%	16%
No income	1%
Don't know/refused to answer	7%

Bankrate

32

The Concept of Lifestyle Inflation

Life is certainly not a bed of roses, and an inability to rightfully recognize and accept your life situation can lead to you overstating your financial expectations. It is always a wise thing to manage lifestyle inflation so that you do not go overboard with your expenses and can stay on track. Now, what do we mean by "lifestyle

---

32 https://image.cnbcfm.com/api/v1/image/105068140-Bankratesavings.png?v=1529477755

inflation?" It is a common phenomenon that with an advance in one's career and salary raise, a corresponding upgrade in lifestyle is inevitable. However, little do we realize that lifestyle inflation can be harmful in the long run as it curbs our saving appetite and even hinders the rate at which we build our wealth. Every extra dollar that you spend to step up your living standards means fewer dollars available ten years down the road or at the time of your retirement.

That is what I mean when I say that you need to understand your current limitations and know how to assess your resources. I say *"current limitations"* because, in the complex world we live in, there are always changes. Personal and professional development goes hand in hand with generous spending habits and ultimately translates to increased financial independence. However, do keep in mind that would require you to sacrifice on the ratio of your savings.

Don't give in to impulsive buying

There's a fine line between needs and wants, which often gets blurred when expenses are not rationalized, and people get involved in irrational spending habits. Being mindful of your expenses is extremely important because it inculcates better spending and saving habits.

Know that needs are absolute necessities that you cannot survive without, such as shelter, food, healthcare, transport, and other related day-to-day expenses. However, wants are things that you have developed a desire for and can do pretty well without.

People often get inspired by successful business owners and start dreaming about owning a similar lifestyle of their own. However, not everyone is born with a golden spoon in their mouth, and you need to realize that sooner or later, you will have to assume responsibility for your life's decisions and actions. Similarly, the carefree college life might seem very attractive to those who are stuck in a rut and are unable to live life on their terms. Success is multi-faceted, and what might appeal to you on the face of it might not necessarily be that way. Everyone has their definition of success, and they maneuver their way through life accordingly.

For a college student, a successful class project might be a milestone. For a 9 to 5 worker, meeting the monthly sales target would be an achievement, whereas a budding entrepreneur might be hoping that he can extend his risk appetite in the next quarter.

The journey towards financial independence is subjective, and it takes a great deal of both intrinsic and extrinsic motivation to not be let down by life's setbacks and take each day as it comes. While some people may be weighed down by parental responsibilities, others are busy handling health issues while others are bogged down by student debt loans, personal loans, auto loans, and mortgages. In the end, everyone has to fight their own battles, and for that, you need to carry out a holistic audit of your strengths and weaknesses so that you capitalize on them to secure your future.

A great way to manage your assets and work toward concrete goals, no matter how big or small, is to leverage your strengths to the best of your ability and build with the resources you have that are tangible, not those that you *wish* you had before you have secured them. Take a look inside yourself and evaluate the tendencies that can propel you forward in life rather than becoming a reason for your failure.

Conclusion

Identify your zone that will highlight your key skills, expertise, and strengths. You must never undermine your efforts. Seize the day by availing every opportunity that comes your way, and learn from your mistakes. Start saving early so that your financial mistakes ultimately mature you into a well-rounded individual with a keen sense of wisdom and financial prudence. Take up something you are most passionate about and see your life turn around in no time. Sign up for vocational training or short courses that will help hone your skills as an individual, take the leap of faith and move to a new city with better opportunities, explore new avenues by exploring your hidden talent, or just start a venture of your own.

Remember, financial independence and freedom do not dawn upon you overnight but is a slow, transformative process that sets you up for long-term sustainable success. Take advantage of financial freebies such as company pension plans, individual retirement accounts (IRA), and dividends from stocks and capital gains. Your

life's financial trajectory is in your hands. Build
a strong foundation to reap the fruits of your hard
work in the long run.[33] [34]

---

[33]
https://www.investopedia.com/terms/e/employer_sponsored_plan.asp
[34] https://www.investopedia.com/terms/i/ira.asp

Chapter 8
Plan for Tomorrow

"The best preparation for tomorrow is doing your best today."

-H. Jackson Brown, Jr.

I am the kind of person who believes in working hard for the future and reaping the fruits of one's labor. I want to be able to stand firm and confident and fend for myself without having to rely on anyone for my financial stability or struggling to make ends meet. That's the reason why I try to direct my energies into building my assets and pushing more items into the "*balance*" column.

We are so engrossed in the fast-paced lives that we have. We mindlessly spend on whatever we wish for and desire without taking the time to stop in our tracks and tally our assets and liabilities. What we don't realize is that with the help of some pre-planning, calculated risks, and proper saving strategies, you can turnaround your current financial state. We are in a constant state of frenzy, aiming to achieve the maximum in a limited amount of time. The last thing on our mind is saving for retirement, and we keep on procrastinating our saving plans later into the future. As aspiring individuals working in a corporate role or an entrepreneurial setup, we are so busy building wealth that we do not think of how much time we waste.

Likewise, we don't pay heed to the times to come when these zealous, passionate years and our career will near its end. Saving for retirement is the last thing on our minds, and over 64% of Americans have less than $10,000 in savings in their account. 45.5% don't even bother thinking about it as they believe that the future will sort itself out. [35]

How Much Money Do Americans Have <u>Saved</u> For
Retirement?

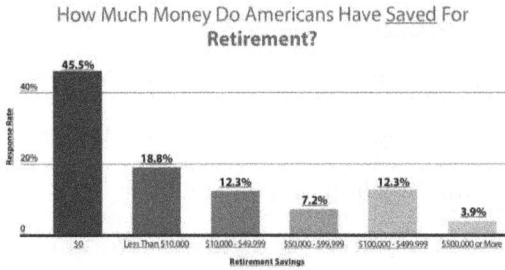

The prospects for Americans seem rather bleak, and that is a cause of major concern. A 2019 survey by GO Banking Rates reveals that a considerable chunk of the millennial generation is expected to retire broke. The common reasons

---

[35] https://www.gobankingrates.com/retirement/planning/why-americans-will-retire-broke/

cited for their hypothesis include:

- An inability to save due to low income
- Excessive debt
- Rent and mortgage payments
- Other expenses as they emerge along the way

When you are in your youth, your energy levels are at a maximum, and you are driven by unprecedented levels of motivation leading to unmatchable levels of productivity. That is the time when you need to channel your skills and expertise in the right direction to make the most of your time.

With age, it is but natural that your mental and physical energies tend to mellow out, and you do not have the same zeal to accomplish things like you used to. Planning well before time is all about keeping your eye on the matrix.

So, think about this: What is contributing to your tangible and intangible assets, and how can you develop them most efficiently? On the other hand, you also need to watch out for the leaks that may be undermining your financial position and adding to your liabilities. Almost two-thirds of millennials have confessed that they live paycheck-to-paycheck and a rather meager 38% feel that they are financially stable enough to manage their expenses.[36] The period between your 20's and 30's is probably the time when you're enjoying the peak years of your freedom.

Most of the people in this category are college graduates and are stepping into the next stage of their adult life. If you're lucky enough to be employed and do not have any major responsibilities to shoulder right now, you have a

---

[36] https://www.cnbc.com/2019/05/10/62-percent-of-millennials-say-they-are-living-paycheck-to-paycheck.html

great opportunity to take the risks that you wouldn't be able to take later on in life.

These years represent the most formative years of your life, and now is the time to face your fears, stand up for yourself, pursue your passions and step out of your comfort zone to reap maximum benefits in the future. You must utilize this opportunity fully to secure a financially stable future. This time is not going to come back. Let me give you my example; I had a seven-figure net worth at the age of 36.

Then I hit a wall, got lost in an economic storm during the 2006 recession that we did not even know the country was in until 2008. I topped that off with a wife and two fantastic kids that motivated me to buy another house, which would cause me to work until my late 50's.

The point that I am trying to make here is that because I secured my finances earlier on in life, I did not have to worry about finances when it came to taking care of my wife and children, and I survived the economic downturn as well. Although the numbers on financial stability are not very promising, it does not, in any manner, deter millennials from curbing their spending habits. In fact, millennials are known to spend around $478 per month on *"nonessential"* expenses such as luxury items, entertainment, dining, and vacations. [37]

If you do things right and start saving at an early age, it won't be long until you have your finances sorted in a methodical manner. This brings us to some crucial reflections that need to be timely taken care of:

Have you ever given serious consideration to your five to ten-year financial plan? Do investment prospects attract you? Do you have

---

[37] http://podcast.farnoosh.tv/

enough savings to last you through a financial emergency? Do you have a long-term saving approach that will provide for your after-retirement years? All these questions might seem intimidating, but there will come a time when you will realize that there is no escape. Therefore, you need to take charge of your financial future.

"The best time to plant a tree was 20 years ago. The second-best time is now."

-Chinese Proverb

Act responsibly at the moment so that you can build a sustainable future for yourself and the upcoming generations without having to go through an emotional ordeal. Whether you have just embarked on your professional journey, are climbing the corporate ladder, or are about to retire, it is essential that you plan sensibly for your future.

Planning for tomorrow begins from envisioning a lifestyle you want at or after retirement. Knowing what you are saving for gives you a sense of direction and purpose to work towards. This is what Steven Covey, the author of the book *'Seven Habits of Highly Effective People'* has put on the list, too. He says, *"Begin with the end in mind."* With our minds being already loaded with information, having a clear vision and path to financial independence will help you live within the safe zone.

It will enable you to achieve individuality and financial empowerment at an early age.[38] Financial independence is not only about saving but spending in the right direction so that you can maximize the value of both your time and money. Here are a few telltale tips that will help you make well-informed investment decisions.

---

[38] https://www.franklincovey.com/the-7-habits/habit-2.html

Tip # 1: Take Advantage of Compound Interest by Investing At an Early Age

When it comes to multiplying your money, compound interest is one of the most powerful tools. However, the power of this tool can only be leveraged over the course of considerable time and does not happen overnight. Compound interest, simply put, is the category of interest that you accumulate when the earning you make on your savings starts compounding on itself.

When you're in your 20's, you don't tend to realize the grave importance of setting aside some money every month for retirement. Let me elaborate on an example that depicts how squandering time away and delaying your saving journey can harm your credit rating and financial standing. Say, for example, you start investing at the age of 20, and you set aside $300 a month.

You keep on the legacy until the age of 60. With an 8% interest rate, you can accumulate over $1 million. However, if you delay your investment plans by a decade and start at the age of 30, you will only save $440,445, which is a humongous loss of $550,000. With only $ 36,000 less in your initial investment amount, the compounded value amounts to quite a lot. With a vision to be financially free in the long-term future, you need to take hold of the reigns before it's too late. The opportunity cost of letting those ten years go by needs to be weighed before making any financial decision.

Tip # 2: Don't Pay for Other People's Assets

Let me set an example of how a liability can be morphed into one of the most positive columns. A young man with a good credit score, a limited amount of liability, and a good debt to income ratio is ready to move into his own place.

He is thinking about renting an apartment about 20 miles from his place of employment.

The place he is looking at will cost $875 per month in rent. He will have a $6.00 per day gas expense due to the distance, which is an additional liability to consider. The full bill will be approximately $995 per month. This would be a number attributed to the "liability" column of the matrix. Now let's do some magic and make this a positive situation.

The young man is asked to consider a condominium that is 4 miles away from the office. The condo is priced at $74,000, and he qualifies for a first-time buyer's mortgage. The down payment required for the purchase is $2,220, and the seller is willing to cover all closing costs.

The monthly mortgage on the property is $332.42. There are some additional homeowner expenses and taxes that push that number up to

$635 per month. The gas that will be used going back and forth to the office is now $6 per *week* or $24 per month, making the total expense of $659.

The fascinating part of this magic formula is that instead of burning the cash in the "*liability*" column, it is building equity in the "*balance*" column. The property is increasing in value at a rate of 5% per year. The interest rate on the property is 3.75%. So not only did the young man decrease his monthly cost from $995 to $659, saving him $336 per month, he also changed a part of his expense into an investment.

The value of his property is increasing by $3,500 per year, and he moves out two years later. He does not sell the condo. Instead, he rents it out at $800 per month. And this way, he creates a positive cash flow while having someone else pay the mortgage on his property instead of him paying the mortgage on someone else's.

Tip # 3: Self-Investment is the Best Kind of Investment

One thing in your life that you have complete control over is yourself. And when we speak of investments, the best kind of investment is what you invest into building yourself. But why do we think that this is so important? Well, just like the state of the stock market or bitcoin value, there are many factors in life over which you have no control. But when you invest in yourself, you invest in something you can fully control and count on.

If, for example, you pursue a degree, you can always thrive if you know how to keep furthering your skills as an individual. Working towards enhancing your personal and professional expertise is one of the most worthwhile investments that you could ever make. This is the kind of venture that will never go to waste, and its value will only increase with time. Pursue your passions and acquire a new certification that will equip you with the competitive edge to leave a mark in the industry that you are serving.

Not only will polishing your skills help you land your dream job, but it can also secure you a position in your favorite line of work and establish your credibility. The more proficient your knowledge and skill set, the higher your earning potential will be. This will put you in an advantageous position of earning a decent income for yourself and ultimately setting yourself up for long-term sustainable savings.

Being financially independent ultimately empowers you to pursue things in life that you love and are most passionate about. Financial planning is a holistic, multi-faceted process that helps the individual build wealth over a span of time. Inculcating financially responsible spending habits and bringing specific lifestyle changes is the key to doing this the smart way.

Once you are in the right place financially, it will automatically translate into a better version of yourself spiritually, emotionally, and physically as well.

Tip # 4: Invest in Assets and Avoid Liabilities

Do you know the premise on which rich people operate? They do not spend blindly on luxuries. They are always on the lookout to make more money so that they can afford the luxuries they've always wished for themselves. For example, you buy a piece of property and earn monthly by renting it out. Once you have generated enough profit out of it, you can use it to buy your favorite car or even move into a more spacious home. Likewise, you can also buy another property and rent it out to improve your financial position.

This strategy teaches us one thing: Instead of increasing your liabilities, it's better to develop your assets and then invest them into something more viable. Successful, wealthy entrepreneurs are always looking for opportunities to invest. Even big business owners have a side income to generate enough cash to invest back into their businesses.

It is always advisable to retain some of your earnings so that they can be invested, multiplied, and utilized to fund the expenses of your business. There's a concept known as the 'Wealth Triangle' that elaborates on the three most important elements that make it up. These include high-income skills, scalable business, and high-paying investments. [39] Technology has practically revolutionized the way we work together as well as in teams, and this has

---

[39] https://www.youtube.com/watch?v=hjgN-K_b7nk&t=418s

accelerated revenue generation by a great deal. So, why don't we look for ways to multiply our money and save to drive toward a more sustainable and financially secure future?

Tip # 5: Build On Short-Term Goals to Achieve Long-Term Goals

Young investors often get intimidated by long, extended timelines and are unable to plan whether they will be able to save for that long to build up their wealth consistently. With so many uncertainties surrounding us in this fast-paced world, it is natural to feel insecure, and hence, setting short-term goals is one way to go about it.

Prioritize the liabilities that need to be paid off on an immediate basis, followed by less pressing issues and then those that can wait. Once you have accomplished your short-term goals, move on to slighter bigger ones. Set new benchmarks and best practices to achieve bigger goals. Do not be let down by failures, for they are what shape who you are and help you develop a far-sighted vision by making you gain experience. Research shows that people who plan ahead and have a proper strategy in place to build wealth are more successful in the long run than people who don't.

SMART goals help bring you closer to your dreams and make your financial plans more executable. Bounding your financial liabilities within timelines pushes you to get rid of them as per the planned schedule. Being goal-oriented organizes you and puts you in greater control of your life – both financially and mentally.

Planning for a financially promising and stable future requires one to be very patient and think realistically. Do not abandon your saving and spending habits midway and follow your financial resolutions religiously. If your goals feel elusive at any point in time, resort to other alternative ways of saving but never abort the mission completely. Realistic planning is all about understanding the situation and the need of time. It requires you to practice moderation in a way such that you do not go overboard with your budgets while also not missing out on the fun element in life.

In short, balance is essential so that you do not find yourself in financial doldrums. It's all about how you strike the perfect balance on the road to financial independence. Calculated risks are never harmful. For you to be able to build wealth, you need to proportionally increase your risk appetite and assess the short-term volatility of certain investments that can give you good returns in the near future. These risks could be anything from investing in a risky stock or bond, taking the leap of faith when undertaking a new career, switching jobs, or bringing about a change in your lifestyle. Always remember that any spending and saving experiences help you learn and grow professionally as well as financially. On the face of it, you might be losing out on financial gains.

But you will have acquired financial literacy and prudence to make better, well-informed decisions in the future. According to research, 24% of millennials are known to show basic financial literacy, while those who fare higher on finance knowledge is only 8%. However, 69% of millennials rate themselves high on possessing a sound knowledge of their finances. [40]

---

[40] https://www.financialimpulse.com/personal-finance-statistics/

Chapter 9
Teach How to Fish If You Have to Feed Those Close to You

The cycle of financial dependence is a vicious one. It all starts very innocently, out of goodwill, and a sincere intention to help someone, more often a family member, out. It can be your child, a sibling, your very own parents, or even a distant relative seeking out your financial help. You generously extend a helping hand.

During times of shortage of cash or a restrictive budget, it is but natural that you turn towards your family members and loved ones to help you out. Nobody knows what the future holds for them. A financially debilitating situation can bring you to the brink of bankruptcy. Bills go unpaid, debt tends to pile up, and the effects trickle down to family members who voluntarily take up the responsibility of helping their loved ones. In the process of trying to improve someone's financial condition, you unconsciously commit to an obligation. Seeing your family members struggle with their finances can be very heartbreaking. As much as you want to help them to the best of your abilities, there are always specific time and financial constraints that will limit your capacity to do so.

Your funds and timelines also matter. You cannot take ardent steps in the heat of the moment and face the repercussions later on in life. The 'Society of Actuaries' recently conducted a survey which revealed that Americans consider it their duty to help their family members in need of financial assistance. Furthermore, a survey conducted by "Family Obligations Across Generations" shows that two in five Americans have extended financial support to a family member in the past year. [41] Wanting to help your loved ones is only natural and is a sign that you care for them. However, from a financial perspective, you would want to review your plans. The rising cost of living, insanely high educational expenses, and staggering student debt have put all of us in a difficult financial position.

Hence, turning to family becomes critical. Not only do parents support their children, but even the millennial generation doesn't step back from assuming the responsibility of their aging parents. Nonetheless, jeopardizing your finances in the process is not the solution. According to a study, one in five Millennials is supporting their aging parents, which amounts to almost $18,250

Chapter 1 [41] Taylor, M, (2019), *Supporting Family Members in Need Without Risking Your Own Financial Future* annually. [42] If you feel you are stuck in a tight spot when it comes to providing financial assistance to your loved ones, here is what you need to do:

- Assess your financial position first. Reflect on your savings and consider whether you are in a sound space to loan out or lend money. Is the problem at hand temporary or pervasive? Does the dependent have a future contingency plan to cover up the loopholes?

- Communicate your expectations if you decide to help the person in financial distress. Decide the terms of repayment, if any. It is important because deciding early on keeps the expectations clear for both parties involved in such a situation.

---

[42]Lamberti, P, (2019), *How To Help Your Parents Financially — Without Going Broke Yourself*

This, in turn, helps keep relationships safe by keeping the air clear since the very start.

- If you want to help the person going through tough times immediately, assess all the cash and non-cash ways to help. Your help can be in the form of cash, paying off bills and dues, extending a loan, or giving a gift card, etc. It doesn't necessarily need to be a temporary transfer of funds.

- Provide the resource or create a job opportunity for them. This will not only help them offset their short-term goals but improve their financial standing in the long-term as well. You could even introduce them to training and counseling programs to help them pave out a way for future income generation.

In this manner, you don't really help them financially but pave the way for them to improve their overall financial standing and thrive. The purpose of including this chapter here is to present the idea that direct financial help is not the only help you can give to your loved ones. There are several other ways you can improve their financial situation without making it all about the money that you lend. In fact, when you give them money in any form, you make them unnecessarily dependent on you.

Financial dependency in adulthood may lead to dire consequences such as chronic and debilitating reliance on others and a dishonorable propensity for evading financial responsibility. People tend to get laid back and do not step out of their comfort zone to take up tasks as technically; they are not "paying the bills." This may breed a sense of lethargy and pleasure-seeking, curbing growth, and personal development. In that case, you are under pressure not only financially but emotionally as well.

Hence, you must not only help people by giving monetary or non-monetary favors to curb the crisis. You need to take up the additional responsibility of creating opportunities that are long-term and sustainable.

It is recommended that you equip the financially dependent person with the tools to take control of their expenditures. It's not that you are not willing to help the other person, but you also need to consider your financial matrix. Also, if you only give them the money to make it through, it will only last for a defined period of time.

After that, they will be in crisis again, and the cycle will keep repeating. Imagine a scenario where you can empower someone financially while strengthening your finances. Suppose your parents are living on rent, and they have to pay

$800 every month. Now, because of their financial constraints, they can only pay $600, which is $200 less than the total amount of rent, so you decide to pitch in. What you are doing is taking money from your "*balance*" column and adding to your "liability" column. Does this make money that could be used as an investment turn into money used as an expense - short term help that will have a long-term cost to you? Instead of diverting your potential positive asset to create an additional liability, what you can do is set aside some cash to purchase a condo with a mortgage of $500 to $600 per month.

You can shift your parents into this condo and charge them a rent amount of $600, which they can afford. This way, you will be empowering them with a feeling of self-worth, and they wouldn't feel financially indebted to you. Moreover, you will not be incurring the $200 liability that you were previously doing. **When** managing my own finances, I try to avail every opportunity to appreciate my assets when helping out a loved one. This way, I am also strengthening my financial health. Although this is a very situation-specific example, what I intend to convey is that you can extend financial help while keeping people responsible and preserving your savings. There must be some skill or asset that they can capitalize on to come up with a long-term sustainable plan to pay off their financial obligations. All they need is a perspective to see through their hidden talents and put their skills to use.

The feeling of obligation can cloud your judgment and lead you to the financial crisis. All of us want to help those that are close to us. We also want to respond to the cries for help from our friends, family, and sometimes associates. But we need to realize that we can't always be their life saviors. We need to define our financial boundaries and get people to respect them. Otherwise, it won't be long before you find yourself in a financial crunch. This is one place we do not want ourselves to be. It not only puts a dent on our budget and funds but also takes a toll on our emotional, mental, and physical health.

"You can save no one by pulling them into a sinking boat."

To understand this better, imagine that you are on a boat in the middle of the sea. There are 13 people in the water around the boat, and they are drowning at the rate of one every ten minutes. There is a hole in the boat that needs space and time to be repaired, which is approximately 30 minutes. The decision rests in your hands.

What do you do?

Start pulling people into the boat or repair the boat?

You cannot do both.

Many people will try to figure out how they can pull people into the boat while fixing it, but that is not an option. Fix the boat or load the boat. You may be tempted to pull people into the boat, and this will end in everyone drowning since the boat needs repair to stay afloat. If you spend the same time (that you spend towards saving people) in mending the boat, you would be able to save more people. The boat will be repaired in 30 minutes, and by then, three people would drown but ten, and you would be saved.

The takeaway here is to conduct a cost-benefit analysis of saving people first vs. mending the boat. If you keep adding people to the boat without mending it, the chances are that the boat would eventually sink because of the undue pressure.

The lesson to learn here is that you need to first carry out a holistic analysis of your financial position before helping your loved ones. Helping out others at the risk of your own family's financial stability is definitely not a wise thing to do. Only when you are financially stable enough yourself can you make space for others to fit in on your schedule and budget. If you jeopardize all that you have and add additional responsibility to yourself, the whole foundation may collapse.

Conclusion

People don't usually prefer doing business with friends, but I would rather not mix family and money either. However, when the going gets tough, and your loved ones experience financial turmoil due to uncertainties of any sort – they are likely to reach out to you. Before you make any commitment, consider your financial position.

Weigh the pros and cons of getting into this financial obligation and make sure that you are on the same page before extending a loan. Also, keep in mind that it is better to help your loved ones by creating opportunities or working out long-term solutions for them than just giving money or loans.

This could be in the form of creating job opportunities or a small business that you can finance that can help them meet their financial needs. There is no better way to become financially sound than to think of ways that will generate sustainable results in the far-lying future.

Chapter 10
Understand the Game
You're Playing

Time is money, and money buys time.

Time and money are inextricably linked. Time is the most precious commodity in today's fast-paced world. The contemporary lifestyle is very demanding, and although time doesn't come with a price tag – it's something we crave for the most.

Why is it that we expend our energies and spend more than half our day toiling at our workplace or draining our mental energy at our desks? We tend to forget why we dedicate such a large part of our lives to getting up early every morning and leaving our home and family to go to work. We have lost our true selves in a mindless routine, living robotic lives without really understanding the purpose of our existence.

At times, we are lost in the shuffle and addicted to the rat race without really thinking about the track we are running on. It seems like an endless road. Or even worse, coming to a dead-end, not knowing what to do. That's the nature of life. It may look like we know what we are doing when, in reality, we are trapped in a vicious cycle.

There are those that fall off the edge, then others who live to work, and finally, those who work to live. Some people are driven by an undying passion for working day in and day out. Their lives revolve around work, and there is nothing that they would trade it for.

Others work at their bare minimum and only work at a pace that would help them to survive. Finding the balance between these two roles requires a good sense of who you are and where you want the finish line to be. As per the Organization for Economic Cooperation and

Development (OECD), a total of 11% of employees around the globe work for 50 plus hours a week. This is the same for U.S. workers. 63% of peoples' time worldwide is dedicated to *"personal time,"* and that includes the time you want to sleep.[43]Like in business, an exit strategy is a great anchor in routine life as well.

I know people who could endlessly talk about how much they love their job, how their lives revolve around doing justice to it, and how it is at the center of their existence. It's like their entire purpose is driven by getting things done for the organization. Now I know there will be those that talk about how they love their jobs and how much it is a part of their very being. I also know some whose identity is indistinguishable from their occupation. It is an integral part of their personality. Americans are roughly divided into

---

[43] Kolakowski, M, (2019), '*What It Means to Live to Work*'

two groups – one who consider their job as a meaningful part of their life and the others who rely on it for more. 51% of U.S. workers feel that they attach a sense of identity to their jobs. While 30% of Americans only consider their occupation as *"just a job to get them by, "*[44] I am talking about those that may have more of a job rather than a career.

They have chosen careers so that they can afford a decent lifestyle and even some luxuries. Most of us go to work to make money. Extrinsic motivation is what usually drives us to get up and go to work every day. Money that we use to send our kids to school, to buy beautiful gifts, purchase groceries, take a relaxing trip to the mountains and pay our rent or mortgage. Unfortunately, there are times that we go beyond

---

[44]." Vojinovic, I, (2019), *'Job Satisfaction Statistics: Keep Your Workers Happy and Your Business Healthy'*

that when we don't just buy what we need, we buy what we want. Here, we need to evaluate what you want from life. That said, let's take a look at it from a different angle. I have mentioned several times that money is time, and time is money. The next time you go shopping or out to a nice dinner, look at the bill and translate the dollars into minutes or hours.

If you are making $15 per hour and you go out for a dinner that costs $75, followed by a $79 show, you are investing just over 10 hours of your productive time in exchange for the 3-hour night out. If you are making $12 an hour and you are paying someone to watch your child that is charging $8 per hour, you are actually reducing your hourly rate to $4.

That is because your time is being offset by someone else's time that you are buying. An economist named Daniel Hamermesh, in his book, *"Spending Time: The Valuable Resource"* elaborates on the concept that people who have a high income, tend to work harder and for longer hours. This is because they feel rushed to make more money and spend accordingly.[45] It might defy common sense, but psychologically, the better off you are in terms of monetary wealth, the more time pressure you feel. Someone who can afford to spend their leisure time by booking a night at the theatre as opposed to a person who would rather curl up in bed and binge shows on Netflix. Not only is the latter person saving up on money, but he doesn't feel the time pressure either. This is exactly what Daniel talks about in his book, *"Time Stress."*

Time can be conveniently exchanged for money when we want to outsource our chores to free up time. The people whose services help

---

[45] Meltzer, L, (2019), '*The Relationship Between Time, Money And Productivity'*

with your home maintenance, vehicle repair, babysitting, medical assistance, tattoos, or dry-cleaning are charging you for their time to complete those services. Most high-end professionals actually bill you by the hour, such as an attorney, psychologist, or life coach. Even your mechanic is charging you for his time plus the cost of the materials he uses to fix your problem. All this is to simply say that the more you spend, the more time you have to invest to cover the bill. Think about this relationship the next time you are deciding whether you want to buy time at the rate others are selling it or if it is more cost-effective to do it yourself.

I am not saying that you should not enjoy life and a nice dinner every now and then. My only suggestion is that in order to keep the budget well-adjusted to your personal money matrix, it is advisable to know how much time it costs you. Most people never really consider the relationship between time and money. These two elements in our society are blood brothers. Even our justice system penalizes you by taking away your time and or fining your monetary amounts. The search for money drives the destitute while the desire for more time drives the rich. Isn't it ironic that we are always running after something we don't have? However, we all live by the same clock. Have the same 24 hours in a day, 60 minutes in an hour, and seven days a week. It's up to us as to how we spend the time we have, which is a constant and to accomplish maximum things in it.

As cliché as it may sound, *"time is money."* You can justifiably associate time to be a valuable currency. It's like every day, 24 hours gets deposited in your "bank account." You have the liberty of letting them go or spending them lucratively to develop your assets so that you can improve your quality of life.

"Lost time is never found again."

-Benjamin Franklin

Make Your Time More Valuable

Time is an intangible asset that you cannot afford to waste. One of the essential traits of a successful person is their ability to value and respect time. However, at some point in time, we are all guilty of wasting time in unproductive activities such as binge-watching shows on Netflix or scrolling mindlessly on social media.

Ideally speaking, your free time should be spent doing stuff that adds value to your life. This can include physical exercise, learning a new language or skill, volunteering for a social cause, budgeting your finances, or organizing your schedule for the week. One way to get started is to plan how you want to spend your days and take the bigger picture into perspective. Self-education is a great way to increase value.

Let me explain it to you with the help of an example. If you own a business and you keep on repeating the same business processes without any reengineering or innovation, a time will come when those practices will become obsolete. Thereafter, investing the same time as you did wouldn't give you the same return on investment (ROI) five years down the road.

Here's a different way of approaching it: Learn ways to eliminate any conflicts that might be undermining your productivity. Are there any technological advancements that could speed up operations? Can you implement a business management theory to optimize business goals?

There are unlimited avenues to explore if you want to make your time more valuable. Self-education and learning is one such avenue to accelerate the achievement of monetizing your time. The average American is known to read only 12 books a year, whereas a CEO reads over

50 books in the same time period. [46]Now, folks, that is the reason for their prestige and fame. They continuously invest in themselves to improve their knowledge-base and skill set.

Of course, the more proficient you are and capable of performing your job in a reduced amount of time, the more valuable your time is. Most jobs have a standard and basic expectation about how productive an hour is. The rate they pay for that position is based on that standard.

If you find yourself being able to complete twice the amount of work that is expected, you may want to cash in on the fact that you are providing a multiple for your time. My life has been a series of experiences where I have learned to upscale businesses and have gained proficiency in structuring them. I started with

---

[46] https://www.capablewealth.com/rich-people-buy-time-poor-people-waste-time/

collaborating with small businesses and enterprises and then went on to work with corporate giants and limited liability companies. I then went on to secure state and local business licenses and working my way through the various offices that needed to approve a new business. I was also very competent at working things out with general contractors, planning, and the local health district. I later leveraged my knowledge to assist other small business entrepreneurs who found my proposed business strategies to be a great money-saving paradigm when it came to the opening and registration of a new business.

I charged almost twice as much as other consultants, and when my potential client questioned my rate, I gave them their first consultation for free. That first consultation consisted of a simple mathematic analysis. This is how it goes: Get your business prospectus put together, seek approval, and start the process within approximately 10 hours. I give approximately five hours of my billable time, which will include getting your bylaws outlined. I should be able to set up an initial appointment with the proper agencies for your sales tax, business license, and your workmen's compensation requirements in another hour.

So, all in all, we are looking at approximately 16 hours. Contrast that with another consultant, who charges half my rate, however, exerts three times the amount of time to carry out the same tasks. So you will be paying him/her for 48 hours while only paying me for 16. That means that even though I "cost more," I will actually save you 16 hours of paying for him for eight of my hours doing the same work.

This is what I explain to my clients. That is also the way I can double the value of my time by accurately appraising my services. You see, it's about how well you utilize time. Accurately assessing the value of a product, service, or your own time is a skill shared by few. I have been employed on more than a few occasions to do just that. This is something that can change your financial dynamics substantially. Start by analyzing the details of the process when you are assessing the value of your services. It is not only about the time invested but also about any potential opportunity lost.

What tools do you need to complete the task successfully? What liabilities are you taking on by agreeing to provide the services? These are the expenses that you will incur. Next, what type of asset are you providing the person receiving your services? How does the time you're investing effect the "money-time" matrix of the person receiving your services? Let me provide a practical example: your associate from the gym finds out that your kids attend two different schools that are very close to each other. He proposes that you provide him with a car service and take his kid to school when you're taking your own kid in the morning. He explains that he has a time constraint, and taking his kid to school cuts into his potential income, causing him to lose $120 a day. What is your time worth, and how can you add to your income bracket? The cost to you is the added stress of making sure that you are able to get both kids to school at the same time.

You also have considered that you are responsible for the well-being of the kids while they are with you. You must also leave home sooner to make sure you are able to pick up and drop off both kids on time. You are paying for the gas, maintenance, and consumption of the car you use. That is one side of the coin. Importantly, consider the other side of the coin or the "cost." Then ask yourself what the cost is? He makes $120 more per day, thanks to your service. You make $20 an hour, and it will require you to invest an additional 30 minutes each morning to pick up the second child. Without considering the details, you may think your services are worth $10. However, considering all of the details, I would posit that $30 per trip is a fair price. The client still comes out $90 ahead, has less wear on his vehicle, and has lowered his fuel costs.

The crux of the entire discussion is how well you can strike the perfect balance when incurring additional costs, without undermining your financial life and saving your "stress boat" from capsizing. Recent research published in the "Proceedings of the National Academy of Sciences Journal" shows that a higher level of happiness was associated with spending on a time-saving purchase rather than a materialistic buy. [47]

"If you need one person to believe in you, be that person."

I have often observed that innovative thinkers and creative entrepreneurs do not give themselves the credit that they deserve. They need to reward themselves for gathering the guts to challenge the status quo and break out of the 9 to 5 routine. Cheering for yourself boosts your morale and fills you with increased passion and a true sense of love and appreciation. It helps you live life meaningfully, with gratitude and fulfillment. I know people frequently need a cheerleader to motivate them when it comes to competitive environments.

It is easy to simply say "yes" without conviction. It is also easy to sell things for free.

---

[47] Harris, E (2017), '*Study Shows Time Is The Most Valuable Commodity. So Here's A Smart Way To Value Time'*

At least, most of the time it is. This is an obstacle that you can overcome if you understand it. There are usually several sides when it comes to a game. That is if you're not playing solitaire. However, even then, it is you against a chance. When you're playing, don't waste your time playing to lose. Play to win and understand that the other side is doing the same. You have to be your *own* advocate, cheerleader, and champion. You need to check-in with yourself before you check in with the world. Being your own cheerleader is not boasting that you are better than the rest, but it's about honoring your journey.

You have to appraise your value. Evaluate your worth and prove it to the other party and establish your price on fair terms. Now it is "game on" and you must play to win. Winning does not mean you get everything you expect or want. It means you emerge as the clear winner on true merit.

You end up with more than you started with. Even better yet, you leverage your position to maximize your potential. Advocate for yourself, do not worry about others as they will advocate for themselves. I see people going the extra mile to publicize their opponents, knowingly or unknowingly. That is not the way to win the game. When we start to think of ourselves as an indispensable ally, comrade, and, eventually, a cheerleader, we forge a deep internal bond with ourselves. We can count on ourselves in unimaginable and inspiring ways.

"I am the greatest. I said that before I even knew I was."

-Muhammad Ali

Chapter 11
What Does It Mean To You

Everyone has a different and unique relationship with money. The path that you take to attain, spend, and manage it is dependent on two major aspects. One: the way you are raised through childhood and the values ingrained in your value system at that time. Two: the way you process and organize information in your head. Knowing why you use money the way you do will help you manage your capital.

We went over this briefly in chapter one. You need to be consciously aware of the different areas and the percentage of the income that you need to dedicate to each sector. Say, for example, you spend 30% of your total income on food and groceries, 20% on transport, and the rest you divide between leisure, recreation, and an emergency fund. When you consciously know beforehand how much to dedicate to each sector, you automatically train your mind to allocate money accordingly. Everyone does not have the same type of relationship with money, so the way they use it may vary greatly. You need to do some self-investigation and try to find out how you feel about money at the core. Why do you get up and go to work every day looking for a check once or twice a month?

Once you get that check, what do you do with the funds you have received? A lot of people have just become a part of the status quo. They go to work to earn money without any other type of justification or reason. They are not fulfilled by their jobs; they are not making any major changes to society or even their immediate communities. In fact, the Millennials are known to be the *"student debt generation"* as compared to Gen Xers, who are known for non-essential spending. So, instead of contributing to the wealth pool, they owe money to the economy. U.S. households owe $1.6 trillion worth of student loans, which is 150% higher than in 2006. [48] They are investing time into something that has no more meaning for them then the pay they receive for the time they invest. If they are not working for the joy of the work they are doing, then they are working for the money. That money is used to fill that void. That void is comfort, security, and power. It is a sense of importance or belonging. A lot of times, money is the key people use to fill this void.

"Money has never made a man happy yet, nor will it. The more a man has, the more he wants. Instead of filling a vacuum, it makes one."

-Benjamin Franklin

---

[48] Dynarski, (S, (2019), *'Student Debt'*

Your Relationship with Money

If you are someone struggling to get your money plan right, you should sort out your core money values. Many of you might have an internalized value system, but you haven't taken out the time to reflect on them and incorporate them into your financial plans. It is also possible that your relationship with money has changed over time due to income and lifestyle changes. Hence, you must revisit your core values in order to align them with your financial needs.

Once you have your values laid out in front of you, start tracking down your purchase history. Use a budgeting app or copies of your past bank statements to delve deeper into your spending habits. Make sure to tally each item against an internalized core value. This will also help you identify the cracks and crevices that are responsible for leaking your income unnecessarily. As a result, you can address your money problems and get on with fixing your finances.

"You hope for the best; I'll save for the worst."

So, the question you should ask is what money does for you. Does it make you feel safe? Do you use money as a safety blanket that allows you to deal with unforeseen issues that pop up? Is it comforting for you to have a response to the car breaking down, the kid that breaks an arm or the washing machine that decides to go on strike?

I am a bit this way. I spend conservatively, and it makes me feel good to be able to have some reserves to use when the unexpected comes up. Such a person is good at not spending more money than they can afford, usually has good credit, and lives within their means.

Success is based on how much they can put aside, not how much they are able to spend. People who maintain such a relationship with money tend to be stressed by the lack of it.

Ironically, they always lack money, and they always will even if they have more than the average American. That is because they are always calculating their financial needs.

This dollar amount equals this amount of tuition; the babysitter offsets this amount of earnings. Those who go by the "safety blanket" money approach are wary of how things can affect them financially. They keep track of their spending and avoid spending money they have not yet earned.

Managing money is easier said than done. It perplexes us to the core and pushes us into an abyss of uncertainty and depression. We are told time and again to have control of our finances, yet we continue to fail to do so. The stress that comes with money is real. It is bizarre for people in their late 20s and 30s to blame their parents for poor financial knowledge since the definition has changed drastically over time. The relationship our parents or grandparents had with money was different from the emotions we associate with money nowadays. [49]These people will not take the vacations, go out on the town, and spend thousands or drive the nicest cars unless they can afford to do so.

"Money is the key to what I really want!"

There is yet another category of people that cover up for their loneliness with money. They are consumed with a sense of materialism, desiring more and more luxury and possessions to cover up for the void inside of them. According to research by the "International Journal of Psychology," materialistic people are often lonely at heart. A person that has this type of relationship with money is one that uses money to fill the void with objects and tangible rewards. This person buys toys, takes vacations,

---

[49] Wiseman, E, (2013), *Money Is My Security Blanket – And Sometimes A Mirage*

likes fancy dinners, and does not do much long-term planning. According to a recent survey, Americans today dine out twice as much and own twice as many cars as they did 55 years ago. [50] Money is not as important as what it can buy. Such people feel better when they can treat themselves to nice things. It does not matter how much money they have; they will spend it. This type of person is looking for a way to fill their life with the things they like.

They have no love for money, but they do understand it can be exchanged for what they want. Typically, this type of person has fluctuating credit and very little savings. It is a part of the consumer culture that we are all a part of. Generally speaking, these folks believe they will always make more money.

---

[50] Gregoire, C, (2017), *The Psychology Of Materialism, And Why It's Making You Unhappy*

I have met people who were making $45,000 a month and would call in a panic if their check was one day late. One in three people in the U.S. earning between $50,000 and $100,000 live a paycheck to paycheck life.[51] This is because they have no money to pay the bills and had already spent the money before they even received it. These are also the type of people that use a lot of credit.

They tend to carry a balance on their credit cards even if they could pay it down. They do this because they want to feel like they have money when they don't. A simple review of their money matrix would quickly show that people who fall into this category are subject to unnecessary stress related to money, but not actually from the thought of money itself. It is more about the fact that they need to cover past expenses or cover

---

[51] Turner, S, (2019), *Why Are So Many People Stuck In The Rat Race*

new ones. They need more money so they can spend it. The person with this kind of thinking will most likely always have financial hardships of one kind or another.

They will find it almost impossible to save money. Give them $100,000, and they will start rationalizing the purchases they make shortly after that. They will not be comfortable keeping the money for rainy days. Having money does not satisfy them. Spending money does it for them. Your relationship with money would not improve even if your paycheck increases.

This is because your expectations and desires are directly proportional to your income. Man is greedy for money and always desires for more. When you finally reach the $60,000 mark, you can't stop thinking about how to expand your income to $70,000. Our consumption keeps on increasing. It's like a vicious circle that keeps us trapped.

"People will never be able to stop working until they stop spending everything."

-Scott Alan Turner

"The pen is mightier than the sword if you use it to sign a check."

Money equals power. The one with the most money has the greatest power. At least that is what those who think that money is a power believe. They feel that money gives them the type of capital they need to stand above others. They like to make sure people know they have lots of money and believe that people should respect them due to the money they have.

They want to be held in high regard because of their financial status. Why is it that people like to flaunt the wealth that they possess? The answer is simple; it fills them with a sense of pride that makes them stand out amongst a crowd of people. They like to be the cynosure and want people to look up to them for their material status.

These individuals that use money as a power-play usually need to have lots of it, and most of them do not make it. They are at least one generation away from the actual money makers. They buy expensive luxury cars and take friends to fancy dinners as a status symbol and a display of their wealth. They expect to be treated with respect, not for how they treat others or what they do, but for what they have, *i.e.*, for the power, or should I say for the money that they have.

They gauge their worth in terms of money. As long as they are financially stable, their self-esteem is going through the roof. If you fall into this group, I doubt you would be reading this book. You don't need to know how to manage your money or stretch your resources. That said, you may be trying to get into this group, and you may be having a real hard time at it. If your budget is bigger than your wallet, stress will inevitably creep in. When money is power, you tend to have to spend it to wield it. You buy flashy cars, the type that costs you more than you can afford. You pick up the tab to show you are in charge. It's all a show of wealth. People in this category get a weird kind of satisfaction from showing that they are superior to the others that they dine or hang out with.

Money makes you feel powerful, but the lack of money makes you feel weak. Money practically controls your sense of happiness and satisfaction, but you also tend to fret over the need to receive constant social validation. You are stressed and tend to feel a bit of envy for the things that others have. You are consumed by the notion that the more wealth you possess, the more powerful and successful you are in the eyes of the world. It's human nature to run after material things in life to feel complete and validated. People who fuel their ego and self-esteem by empowering themselves with worldly riches are on the constant quest to keep earning and flaunting their wealth, but their financial stress is something that an average American cannot even fathom.

Hence, the relationship with money is integral in shaping our financial status and security. That's what we have been discussing since the beginning of this chapter. It's how you view money and then relate it to your core values that help you steer your boat in the right direction. Carry out a holistic analysis of what money means to you so that you can better understand your needs and treat them accordingly.

"Never spend your money before you have earned it."

-Thomas Jefferson

Chapter 12
Putting It All Together To Make Dollars Make Sense

All about choices...

Personal finance has its base on a bedrock of choices. Every day is a new opportunity to make well-informed financial choices for a stable future. Every little decision that we make leads to specific financial implications that affect our lives for the better or the worst. The bottom line is; you simply need to get in control to be in control. Life is about choices and actions that cause reactions. Take the proper action, and the reactions will be positive.

Take, for instance, your grocery shopping ritual. Although it is a fundamental day-to-day decision, making mindful choices when deciding what to load into your cart helps you cut down on unnecessary expenses. Similarly, if you are planning to go on a weekend getaway, the destination you choose will be the primary impact on the expense. Still, other choices such as the method of travel, who is coming with you, and what type of experience you want to have will create miscellaneous expenses, irrespective of the destination. Life is full of choices. From small choices to life-changing ones, we all have to make a few every day. With the right mindset and consistency, you can take over your financial responsibilities. Here's what you can do daily to attain your long-term financial goals:

- Prioritize and remind yourself of the goal that you wish to achieve. View each day as a fresh opportunity to work towards your goal and keep reinforcing that mentality.

- Consider using visual reminders and motivators if that helps. What motivates you to make better financial choices? Fill your space with cues that will guide you to live a life where you are in control of our finances.

- Start your day with the most important financial decisions. Your mind is fresh early in the morning, and it is advisable to settle your finances so that you are all set to seize and conquer the day.

- Keep temptations at bay. Change the path of your commute that crosses a coffee shop or a bookstore that entices you to spend your money.

- Lay down your financial roadmap in detail and ask yourself how you intend to go from "Point A" to "Point B." Keep it flexible to accommodate a financial emergency.

- Keep a balance and add a healthy dose of "reality-check time" and to make sure that your plan is free of any loopholes.

Contingency planning is essential.

Above all, you will have to identify what type of relationship you do have with money. If you know what motivates your decisions, you will have greater control over your choices. Know what your goal is. Write it down. Envision the life you wish to have and then make it real.

Prioritize your needs over your wants and consider the long-term effects of your choices. Making responsible choices starts at an early age. According to a 2017 survey, teenagers have quite a good understanding of the concept of finance. Teenagers earn $465 on average per month, and approximately 58% of teenagers intend to take up part-time work during their college years to pay for college debt. [52]

---

[52] Backman, M, (2017), '*7 Stats That Show How Today's Teens Are Making Smart Money Choices*'

"You cannot make a dollar out of 99 cents."

Financial independence does not emerge overnight; in fact, it takes years of toiling, hard work, and consistent financially-sound habits to be successful. As they say:

Take care of the pennies, and the dollars will take care of themselves.

In effect, this principle requires one to take care of the smaller financial issues, and the more pressing ones will be easier to handle. You cannot expect to accumulate a reserve if you have a laid-back attitude when it comes to tracking your small, day-to-day expenses. Managing your money, as an overarching task, requires developing a disciplined mindset. I would like to reiterate that if you learn to control your money that goes into groceries and other day-to-day expenses, managing bigger expenses (like rent, debt, and mortgages) will automatically seem less burdensome.

This is because your brain is wired to approach a minimalistic and money-conserving approach. This will prove to be fruitful in the long run for both you and your future generations. Quite often, I have been teased because I point out the cents when others round up or down to the nearest dollar. I have laughed all the way to the bank when chastised by people who think that a "dollar here" and a "dollar there" is insignificant when managing their personal wealth.

It does not make a difference in their final balance. Remember, you need 100 pennies to make a dollar. Likewise, you need 100 dollars to break a $100 bill. The sum makes the whole. Consider the pennies or the single units, manage some of your money, and soon you will be able to manage all of your money. Small changes go a long way. If you want to be able to pay the down payment for a house, plan for it. If you need $8,000, how long will it take you to secure it? Take $10 each day and move it into a savings account. If you usually spend $16.00 for lunch, bring your lunch and make sure you do not spend more than $6. That is where you will find the $10 you need.

Stop purchasing coffee on your way to work in the morning. Wake up a few minutes early and make your own coffee at home. That saves you another $5 per day, bringing your total daily savings up to $15 per day. That combination alone will allow you to set aside $3,750 per year. If you smoke, cut back. A pack a day costs you over $1,825 per year.

Even if you do not smoke, there is still something that is an unnecessary or extra expense. Such expenses ultimately deter you from getting closer to pursuing big things like owning your own home. You need to prioritize what matters more - these small splurges or the ultimate dream house? Reduce the car payment or reduce the number of dine-outs per month. That will allow you to set aside $960 to $1,000 per year. Even cutting down on your trash pickup services can save you $500 quarterly, and $2000 in the long haul. Relatively insignificant things, when looked at as the bigger picture, translate into humongous savings.

Think of how if you started monitoring all of the pennies that you spend mindlessly, you'd be in a much better position financially. They all contribute to your final financial standing and make you a better person.

If you are able to save $4,750 per year, it will do two things. First, you will quickly be on the top half of individuals saving in America, and second, you will have your down payment for your home in less than two years.

American households saved a median balance of $7000 in the year 2019. However, the average is highly biased, with the high-income outliers at $30,600. [53]

"Appreciate what is real."

"Without gratitude and appreciation for what you already have, you'll never know true fulfillment."

-Tony Robbins

"If only I had a bigger car, I would be able to travel more conveniently."

"If only I had a higher-paying job, I would be able to enjoy life more."

"If only I had more success or fame, I would be truly happy."

———————————————

[53] Moon, C, (2019), *Average U.S. Savings Account Balance 2019: A Demographic Breakdown*

How many times do we catch ourselves uttering these phrases unconsciously and being ungrateful for what we do actually have? We live in a perpetual state of always wanting more than we have. We can never have enough materialistic possessions. We always want bigger houses, more luxurious cars, and the like. The need can never be satiated. It is human nature to keep wanting more, better, and bigger. What we have lost in the process is true peace and contentment of heart.

So, here is an abstract idea. Stop and appreciate what you have. Appreciate what you have already achieved and embrace what you currently have. We tend to make a lot of impulsive decisions when we find ourselves under the undue pressure of conforming to societal standards of being rich and happy. If you think that only a lack of money causes stress, you are highly mistaken. People with material possessions are always consumed by the unnecessary worry and stress of guarding their wealth and are always involved in money matters. What they do not do is live in the moment. They are preoccupied with a state of frenzy and a mindless race to accumulate more wealth. Enjoy the little achievements and the treasures you have already been able to secure. Appreciate what you have instead of stressing over what you want. More often than not, we do not realize that the things we once desired are now in our possession. Yet, we are consumed by our greed for more. The things you have are things you wanted before you got them. Now you have them, and you no longer appreciate them since you are not deprived of them anymore.

Money is not the sole element that affects your life. If you were to win a million dollars in lottery right now, even then, it would not have the power to change your life-long term. Only you and your mind have the power to change things. You are in control, and no one else. Money is only a vehicle for buying things and allowing you to have more of the things you have also vied for. It's also a matter of perception. Money puts you in a position to add value to your life by taking care of things and people that matter the most to you. If business trips are your priority, you will spend that money traveling to the biggest metropolitan cities. Whereas, if you treasure quality time with your family, you will invest in a family trip to an exotic destination. The same money can be used in drastically different ways.

"Don't trade tomorrow for yesterday."

As tempting as credit may seem, buying on credit can have dire consequences. I see people making decisions that will cost them heftily in the future. When you buy on credit, you are not only borrowing the money but also committing your time in the future. Depending on your credit limit, the funds that you may be allowed might take you on an overspending spree if you do not exercise self-discipline.

To prevent yourself from going over budget, you need to put a cap on your expenses by only spending as much as you can return in one month. Unless you have a crystal ball and know how to make it work, you never know what the future brings. Changes happen; opportunities suddenly arise, but so do accidents.

Live in the moment and appreciate every moment that you have. Live within your means and only go for things that you can afford. Going over and above your budget limit is only going to undermine your financial standing in the long run. Follow the philosophy of planning your expenses around your income and not on the virtual limit that credit lending allows you. The only time you should shop for items you cannot immediately pay for and will, therefore, need credit to cover the costs associated with assets that either increase in value or allow you to be more productive and therefore increase your future earnings.

According to the Federal Reserve, debt due to credit lending amounted to a huge $1.0645 trillion in the first quarter of 2019. [54] This increasing figure is a sign that you need to practice moderation and not be carried away by prospects or enticements that encourage you to buy things on credit.

To look at it from a realistic perspective, nearly everyone faces life situations that require them to borrow money to achieve their financial goals. However, the key is to manage money-related decisions. If credit is used irresponsibly, it can quickly chip away at your financial health.

---

[54] Herman, J (2019), *Average Credit Card Debt Statistics*

Hence, any additions to your financial plan should be made after careful consideration after evaluating all of the pros and cons.

Make bite-size money goals and approach your financial health one step at a time. Set smaller, realistic goals to reap the benefit and set yourself up for long-term financial success.

"Financial independence is to live from the income of your own personal resources."

-Jim Rohn

Appendix
The Big Bang!

As I was wrapping up this book, the world was dealing with a pandemic that was spreading like a fire in a barnyard! Starting in China, daily life morphed into something out of a Dean Koontz novel. The phrase "social distancing" became incorporated into our every-day lexicon. People were suffering from flu-like symptoms that turned deadly for the elderly population and those with preexisting health conditions.

The news started reporting a surge of unprecedented changes. They continued to say that the situation was "fluid." What they meant was that the situation was beyond their control, and they really did not know what the next day would bring. People were getting sick by the tens of thousands and yet continued rationalizing their way out of doing the right thing.

The "right thing" was keeping enough distance between themselves, so the government had the chance to make up the time that they wasted and could develop a medical solution to the problem. This became known as "flattening the curve." First, there was a fear for life, then there was fear of an economic tsunami. The government was concerned with life, but they were also quite bothered by what would happen to the stock market, large and small industries, and the employment of its citizens. This fear was also a part of what slowed down their reaction and their enforcement of social distancing.

Wait a minute; I think I've gone a bit off track. I really did not want to pretend to understand the economic fall-out of COVID-19 better than those tasked with tackling the chore. One of my friends, however, insisted that I provide some common-sense considerations for a sudden and unexpected economic black hole. Everything you knew to be true yesterday is now challenged. You had a job but were just terminated via e-mail. You were making vacation plans and now need to change that to figure out how to get a new job interview. The real kicker is that you are not alone, and this is happening on a massive scale. So, you are competing against everyone, and time is of the essence.

Depending on how much of this book you have applied, you may be one day rich, one month rich, or good for a few years. What is your next step? Don't panic yet; take an inventory. How much capital do you have access to? Let's create a list with a few columns; *assets, capital,* and *liability.*

On the liabilities don't just indicate what the full amount you owe is but also the payments and when they are due. Note where the capital actually is and include credit as capital if you still have access to it. The assets you are listing need to be divided into two groups: those you are willing to sell (in which case you have to determine what they are) and those that you either don't want to or can't part with.

As noted earlier in the book, time is money. Which means money is also time. We are going to need to use our assets, capital, and credit to create time. We have to move fast on the credit side. Once we start to show the symptoms of joblessness, our credit will quickly be affected. So, let's talk about that first. Do you have a HELOC on your property that has available credit? Go get it! Start making as many payments as possible with your credit cards.

If you're banking with the same bank that holds your mortgage or has provided you credit cards, get your cash out and put it into another financial institution. We will call this phase one of our "survival mode." When you're working with your list of liabilities, you will most likely have a mortgage or rent. You will have various bills like utilities, car payments, loan repayments, tuition, etc. We will have to prioritize this list from those liabilities that need to be paid and those we can default on with the least amount of consequences. Yes, I did say, "default." As things get tight, everyone is not going to be paid.

Now let's figure out our timeline. Comparing the list of necessary payments against the available capital and accessible credit we have been able to accumulate, how much time does that translate into? For example, if you have secured $20,000 and your list of liabilities reflects $6,000 in fees and payments you cannot avoid monthly, you have just over three months of money.

Once you have your timeline, you need to get proactive in this *phase two* of "survival mode." Get up to speed in regard to any programs offered to assist with economic distress. Reach out to your creditors and let them know you have recently suffered economic hardship. See if they will work with you and restructure your repayment. They may do loan modifications with you or even defer payments and eliminate late fees. Keep in mind that creditors will be more eager to work with you if there is actually a real potential in them getting their money back. In order for that to be possible, you need to have a source of revenue.

I don't have an easy fix for the lack of income. Managing what you have is one thing, making money is* another. You have to take the time to focus on the way to replace your income. This can be with another job in the same field or reinventing yourself. Selling your assets is a short-term fix that can't be sustained. You need a revenue stream. The best stream is one that can be scaled. This is what I call the "sustainability phase." Only in the final rebuilding phase will you once again worry about your credit score. Your liabilities should be under control. There is a chance that you may have downsized, made the necessary modifications to your lifestyle, and once again, you're on your own two feet— time to get back in sync with your matrix.

Once you "Know Money," you will have "no problems," or at least be on a smarter path to financial and personal freedom. "Knowing your money" is the first step to having "no problems" in terms of money and having financial freedom and liberty. Nobody can guarantee that your financial worries will be eliminated overnight, but in order to set yourself on the path of financial literacy, you need to start taking small steps and increase your knowledge base. Always remember that you never know when you will need to fall back on your contingency plan and make do in the limited finances that you have. Many people end up making rash, financial decisions because they are not aware of the multi-faceted nature of money and how a little homework could have helped them stay strong and upright on a rainy day.

Whether you want to set things straight when it comes to money, get rid of any liabilities, or simply maximize your financial potential – it all begins from acknowledging that things are not going as planned, and you need to start thinking realistically and practically. However, being real doesn't mean that you exhaust yourself in the process and make sure that you practice moderation in your approach. If you 'know your money' since day one you will always stay on top of your money goals. We need to consciously come to terms with the gaps in our financial cycle and acknowledge the problems plaguing us, not to overwhelm yourself but to find sustainable and viable solutions to real-life problems. Stay safe out there, and keep your money matrix healthy!

"It's not how much money you make, but how much money you keep, how hard it works for you, and how many generations you keep it for."

-Robert Kiyosaki

Biography and References

U.S. household income distribution | Statista. (n.d.). Retrieved from https://www.statista.com/statistics/20318 3/percentage-distribution-of-household-income-in-the-us/

$1.5 trillion of US student loan debt has transformed the American dream— Quartz. (n.d.). Retrieved from https://qz.com/1367412/1-5-trillion-of-us-student-loan-debt-has-transformed-the-american-dream/

29.2% of U.S. Households Had Incomes of $100,000+ in 2017 | CNSNews. (n.d.). Retrieved from https://www.cnsnews.com/news/article/t erence-p-jeffrey/292-us-households-made-more-100000-2017

62% of millennials say they're living paycheck to paycheck. (n.d.). Retrieved from https://www.cnbc.com/2019/05/10/62-percent-of-millennials-say-they-are-living-paycheck-to-paycheck.html

64% of Americans Aren't Prepared For Retirement | GOBankingRates. (n.d.). Retrieved from https://www.gobankingrates.com/retirement/planning/why-americans-will-retire-broke/

503 Connection reset by peer. (n.d.). Retrieved January 21, 2020, from https://www.fool.com/the-ascent/credit-cards/articles/study-the-most-wasteful-spending-habits-among-americans/

105068140-Bankratesavings.png (1325×1045). (n.d.). Retrieved from https://image.cnbcfm.com/api/v1/image/105068140-Bankratesavings.png?v=1529477755

Americans are dying with an average of $62,000 of debt—CBS News. (n.d.-a). Retrieved from https://www.cbsnews.com/news/americans-are-dying-with-an-average-of-62k-of-debt/

Americans are dying with an average of $62,000 of debt—CBS News. (n.d.-b).

Retrieved from https://www.cbsnews.com/news/americans-are-dying-with-an-average-of-62k-of-debt/

Americans Get Better About Saving But Still Have Work To Do | Bankrate.com. (n.d.). Retrieved from https://www.bankrate.com/banking/savings/financial-security-0617/

Bankrate: 65% of Americans save little or nothing. (n.d.). Retrieved from https://www.cnbc.com/2018/03/15/bankrate-65-percent-of-americans-save-little-or-nothing.html

Class of 2018's Preliminary Starting Salary Shows Slight Drop. (n.d.). Retrieved from https://www.naceweb.org/job-market/compensation/class-of-2018s-preliminary-starting-salary-shows-slight-drop/

College Pulse | What College Students Think. (n.d.). Retrieved from https://collegepulse.com/

Credit card users rack up over $1 trillion in debt. (n.d.). Retrieved from

https://www.cnbc.com/2017/02/17/credit
-card-users-rack-up-over-1-trillion-in-
debt.html

*digitalhub | Americans spend at least $18,000
a year on these non-essential costs—
Digitalhub.* (n.d.). Retrieved from
https://www.swnsdigital.com/2019/05/a
mericans-spend-at-least-18000-a-year-
on-these-non-essential-costs/

Employer-Sponsored Plan. (n.d.). Retrieved
from
https://www.investopedia.com/terms/e/e
mployer_sponsored_plan.asp

*Expectations vs. Reality: Early Career Salaries
| LendEDU.* (n.d.). Retrieved from
https://lendedu.com/blog/college-
graduates-salary-expectations-realities/

*Financial Wealth—It's Time not Money—CBS
News.* (n.d.). Retrieved from
https://www.cbsnews.com/news/financia
l-wealth-its-time-not-money/

Habit 2: Begin With the End in Mind. (n.d.).
Retrieved from
https://www.franklincovey.com/the-7-
habits/habit-2.html

How America Pays for College 2019 | Sallie Mae. (n.d.). Retrieved from https://www.salliemae.com/about/leading-research/how-america-pays-for-college/

How credit card use differs across the US - Business Insider. (n.d.). from https://www.businessinsider.com/credit-card-use-across-the-us-2018-8

Individual Retirement Account (IRA) Definition. (n.d.). Retrieved from https://www.investopedia.com/terms/i/ira.asp

It's time to get an education on student loan options. (n.d.). Retrieved from https://www.cnbc.com/2015/11/13/its-time-to-get-an-education-on-student-loan-options.html

Living Paycheck to Paycheck is a Way of Life for Majority of U.S. Workers, According to New CareerBuilder Survey—Aug 24, 2017. (n.d.). Retrieved from http://press.careerbuilder.com/2017-08-24-Living-Paycheck-to-Paycheck-is-a-Way-of-Life-for-Majority-of-U-S-

Workers-According-to-New-
CareerBuilder-Survey

Most Americans Are Taking Vacations They Can't Afford. (n.d.). Retrieved from https://www.forbes.com/sites/learnvest/2 017/06/30/most-americans-are-taking-vacations-they-cant-afford/#18fc7868577a

Nearly 40% of Americans can't cover a surprise $400 expense—CBS News. (n.d.). Retrieved from https://www.cbsnews.com/news/nearly-40-of-americans-cant-cover-a-surprise-400-expense/

New College Grads Overestimate Their Salaries by 23 Percent Study Shows | Inc.com. (n.d.). Retrieved from https://www.inc.com/minda-zetlin/college-grads-overestimate-starting-salaries-study-shows.html

News. (n.d.). Retrieved from https://www.nefe.org/press-room/news/default.aspx

Personal Finance Statistics (2020) | Financial Impulse. (n.d.). Retrieved https://www.financialimpulse.com/personal-finance-statistics/

Personal Finance Statistics: How Do You Compare? - Debt.com. (n.d.). Retrieved from https://www.debt.com/statistics/

Research From PurePoint® Financial Shows The American Dream Is Changing As Savings Stagnates. (n.d.). Retrieved from https://www.prnewswire.com/news-releases/research-from-purepoint-financial-shows-the-american-dream-is-changing-as-savings-stagnates-300525715.html

So Money Podcast—Farnoosh. (n.d.). Retrieved from https://podcast.farnoosh.tv/

Student Loan Debt Climbs to $1.4 Trillion in 2019 | Experian. (n.d.). Retrieved from https://www.experian.com/blogs/ask-experian/state-of-student-loan-debt/

The Fed—Consumer Credit—G.19. (n.d.). Retrieved from https://www.federalreserve.gov/releases/g19/HIST/cc_hist_memo_levels.html

The grim reality of millennials who rely on

their parents for money: 'I pay for lunch at work, and I pay for my Netflix account'—MarketWatch. (n.d.-a). Retrieved from https://www.marketwatch.com/story/why-its-time-to-cut-millennials-some-slack-for-being-financially-dependent-on-their-parents-2019-07-16

The grim reality of millennials who rely on their parents for money: 'I pay for lunch at work, and I pay for my Netflix account'—MarketWatch. (n.d.-b). Retrieved from https://www.marketwatch.com/story/why-its-time-to-cut-millennials-some-slack-for-being-financially-dependent-on-their-parents-2019-07-16

The Wealth Triangle^{TM}—Dan Lok's Pioneered Wealth Strategy—How to Invest Like a Millionaire Ep. 2—YouTube. (n.d.). Retrieved from https://www.youtube.com/watch?v=hjgN-K_b7nk&t=418s

Trends in College Pricing 2019 Highlights. (n.d.). Retrieved from https://research.collegeboard.org/trends/

college-pricing/highlights

U.S. Census Bureau QuickFacts: United States. (n.d.). Retrieved from https://www.census.gov/quickfacts/fact/table/US/PST045218

What Does It Mean to Be "Broke" in America? - CreditLoan.com®. (n.d.). Retrieved from https://www.creditloan.com/blog/broke-in-america/

Based on the 153.6 million American wage-earners, as defined by the Social Security Administration

National Financial Well-Being Survey, Consumer Financial Protection Bureau, 2017

Chapter 1 Taylor, M, (2019), *Supporting Family Members in Need Without Risking Your Own Financial Future*

Lamberti, P, (2019), *How To Help Your Parents Financially — Without Going Broke Yourself*

Kolakowski, M, (2019), '*What It Means to Live to Work*'

." Vojinovic, I, (2019), '*Job Satisfaction Statistics: Keep Your Workers Happy and Your Business Healthy*'

Meltzer, L, (2019), '*The Relationship Between Time, Money And Productivity*'

https://www.capablewealth.com/rich-people-buy-time-poor-people-waste-time/

Harris, E (2017), '*Study Shows Time Is The Most Valuable Commodity. So Here's A Smart Way To Value Time*'

Dynarski, (S, (2019), '*Student Debt*'

Elkins, K, (2019), *Here's The Net Worth Of The Average American Family*

Wiseman, E, (2013), *Money Is My Security Blanket – And Sometimes A Mirage*

Gregoire, C, (2017), *The Psychology Of Materialism, And Why It's Making You Unhappy*

Turner, S, (2019), *Why Are So Many People Stuck In The Rat Race*

Backman, M, (2017), '*7 Stats That Show How Today's Teens Are Making Smart Money Choices*'

Moon, C, (2019), *Average U.S. Savings Account Balance 2019: A Demographic Breakdown*

Herman, J (2019), *Average Credit Card Debt Statistics*

www.ingramcontent.com/pod-product-compliance
Lightning Source LLC
Chambersburg PA
CBHW021925190326
41519CB00009B/912